In Favour of Public Space

TEN YEARS OF THE EUROPEAN PRIZE FOR URBAN PUBLIC SPACE

CONSORTIUM OF THE CENTRE DE CULTURA
CONTEMPORÀNIA DE BARCELONA

President
Antoni Fogué Moya

Vice-president
Jordi Hereu i Boher

Director
Josep Ramoneda

EUROPEAN PRIZE
FOR URBAN PUBLIC SPACE

An initiative of

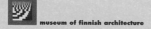

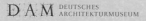

Sponsored by

With the collaboration of

In the context of

IN FAVOUR OF PUBLIC SPACE
Ten years of the European Prize
for Urban Public Space

Published by
**Centre de Cultura Contemporània
de Barcelona and ACTAR**

Direction
Judit Carrera

Edited by
Magda Anglès

Coordinated by
Magda Anglès, Rosa Puig

Graphic Design & Production
ActarBirkhäuserPro

Projects Description
David Bravo

Translations
**Richard Burgess
Discobole
Joseph Ganahl
Robyn de Jong-Dalziel
Julie Wark
Mark Waudby
Branka Žaja**

Proofreading
Mark Waudby

Printed and bound
in the European Union

All rights reserved

© Centre de Cultura Contemporània
 de Barcelona, 2010
 Montalegre, 5
 08001 Barcelona
 www.cccb.org

© ACTAR, 2010

© the authors of the articles
 and the images

ISBN 978-84-92861-38-5
DL B-24348-2010

Distribution
ActarBirkhäuserD
Barcelona · Basel · New York
www.actarbirkhauser.com

Roca i Batlle 2-4
E-08023 Barcelona
Tel. +34 93 417 49 93
Fax +34 93 418 67 07
office@actar-d.com

Viaduktstrasse 42
CH-4051 Basel
Tel. +41 61 2050 777
Fax +41 61 2050 792
sales@birkhauser.ch

151 Grand Street, 5th floor
New York, NY 10013, USA
Tel. +1 212 966 2207
Fax +1 212 966 2214
officeusa@actar-d.com

9
In Commemoration of the Ten Years of the European Prize for Urban Public Space
Antoni Fogué

11
Foreword
Judit Carrera

15
The City and the Human Condition
Josep Ramoneda

24
The Impossible Project of Public Space
Manuel de Solà-Morales

33
Interview with Rafael Moneo
Magda Anglès / Judit Carrera

41
A Decade of Awards
Dietmar Steiner

2010

54
Open-Air Library, Magdeburg
KARO* with Architektur + Netzwerk
TEXT BY Peter Cachola Schmal

60
Norwegian National Opera & Ballet, Oslo
Snøhetta
TEXT BY Kjartan Fløgstad

66
Playa de Poniente Esplanade, Benidorm
Office of Architecture in Barcelona
TEXT BY José Miguel Iribas

72
Fishermen's Huts, Cangas de Morrazo
Irisarri & Piñera
TEXT BY Sarah Ichioka

78
Urban Activators Theatre Podium & Grotekerkplein, Rotterdam
Atelier Kempe Thill
TEXT BY Huib Haye van der Werf

82
Passage 56, Espace Culturel Écologique, Paris
Atelier d'Architecture Autogérée
TEXT BY Francis Rambert

2008

88
Barking Town Square, London
muf architecture/art, Allford Hall Monaghan & Morris
TEXT BY Beatrice Galilee

94
Centrum.Odorf, Innsbruck
Froetscher Lichtenwagner & IDEALICE
TEXT BY Gabriele Kaiser

98
Homage Tower, Huéscar
Antonio Jiménez Torrecillas
TEXT BY Luis García Montero

102
Other People's Photographs, Folkestone
Strange Cargo Arts
TEXT BY Xavier Ribas

2006

108
Sea Organ, Zadar
Nikola Bašić
TEXT BY Željka Čorak

114
A8ernA, Zaanstad
NL Architects
TEXT BY Ole Bouman

120
Piazza Nera Piazza Bianca, Robbiano
Ifdesign
TEXT BY Luca Molinari

124
Heroes of the Ghetto Square, Krakow
Piotr Lewicki & Kazimierz Łatak
TEXT BY Adam Zagajewski

128
Volkspalast, Berlin
TEXT BY Dirk Laucke

44
The Flâneur's Surprise
David Bravo

50
Map of the European Prize for Urban Public Space (2000–2010)
Elías Torres

2004

136
Restoration of the Vall d'en Joan Controlled Landfill Site, Begues
Batlle i Roig Arquitectes + Teresa Galí-Izard
TEXT BY Joan Nogué

142
Refurbishing of the Paseo del Óvalo, Teruel
David Chipperfield, Fermín Vázquez–b720
TEXT BY Luis Fernández-Galiano

148
Harbour Baths, Copenhagen
PLOT A/S: Bjarke Ingels & Julien De Smedt
TEXT BY Lars Gemzøe

152
Tilla Durieux Park, Berlin
DS Landschapsarchitecten
TEXT BY Andreas Huyssen

156
Stortorget, Kalmar
Caruso St John Architects
TEXT BY Philip Ursprung

160
Green Tenerife [Site 9], Buenavista del Norte
GPY Arquitectos
TEXT BY Marina Romero

2002

168
Regeneration of the River Gállego and Environs, Zuera
aldayjover arquitectura y paisaje
TEXT BY Luis Francisco Esplá

174
Lene Voigt Park, Leipzig
Büro Kiefer
TEXT BY Arnold Bartetzky

178
Skatepark in Westblaak Avenue, Rotterdam
dS+V
TEXT BY Hans Ibelings

182
Programme of Urban Rehabilitation in Marinha de Silvade District, Espinho
Sárria-Júnior
TEXT BY Ana Vaz Milheiro

186
Environmental Regeneration of the River Besòs, Barcelona / Montcada i Reixac / Santa Coloma de Gramenet / Sant Adrià de Besòs
Barcelona Regional
TEXT BY Oriol Bohigas

2000

192
Can Mulà, Mollet del Vallès
Serra-Vives-Cartagena Arquitectes
TEXT BY Montserrat Tura

198
Smithfield Public Space, Dublin
McGarry Ní Éanaigh Architects
TEXT BY Shane O'Toole

202
Central Ter Park, Girona
Francesc Hereu & Joaquim Español
TEXT BY Antoni Puigverd

2000—2010

TEN YEARS OF THE EUROPEAN PRIZE FOR URBAN PUBLIC SPACE

Buenavista del Norte
160

In Commemoration of the Ten Years of the European Prize for Urban Public Space

ANTONI FOGUÉ

On the tenth anniversary of the call for entries in the first European Prize for Urban Public Space, the prime cause for satisfaction is the continuity of this idea, a progression marked by growth and consolidation. In instituting this innovative proposal, the Centre of Contemporary Culture of Barcelona (CCCB) aspired to foster recognition of a particular form of city-building through urban planning focused on public space and with citizens, in particular, in mind. Far from being concerned with showcase architecture or landscaping, the aim of the Prize was to call attention to public initiative that, through exemplary collaboration, reached agreement with the talent and creativity of architects.

We can only feel satisfied with this decade of projects that have shaped the successive growing lists of candidates and prize-winners. The aptness of the project is also manifested in the involvement of international partners who have joined the CCCB as co-conveners of the Prize. I should therefore like to express our thanks to The Architecture Foundation (London), the Architekturzentrum Wien (Vienna), the Cité de l'Architecture et du Patrimoine (Paris), the Nederlands Architectuurinstituut (Rotterdam), the Museum of Finnish Architecture (Helsinki) and the Deutsches Architekturmuseum (Frankfurt). These partners have intensified the European vocation that has inspired the initiative of the Prize from the very start because, if we uphold the power and drive of the local governments in a highly globalised society, the European identity constitutes a key element, an essential point of connection that is indispensable in constructing towns and cities that are well rooted in the territory and open to everyone.

In this regard, a glance at the contributions that make up this catalogue of the ten years of the Prize offers a clear illustration of the social vision of the architecture of urban public spaces, of a vocation for public service based on cohesion, social integration and sustainability, and of public action carried out from a standpoint of proximity, promoted by local governments, all of which has a great deal to say when it comes to facing the urban challenges of the future. In sum, it permits us to augur the continuity of this singular and highly prestigious award.

Antoni Fogué is President of the Diputació de Barcelona (Barcelona Provincial Council) and of the General Council of the Centre of Contemporary Culture of Barcelona Consortium.

Foreword
JUDIT CARRERA

Bearing witness to the tensions of public space in Europe: this is the aim of the European Prize for Urban Public Space, which was established in 2000 by the Centre of Contemporary Culture of Barcelona (CCCB). The Prize was an outcome of the exhibition *The Reconquest of Europe* (1999) – with Albert Garcia Espuche as its curator and organised jointly with the then Institut Français d'Architecture – which showed the impressive scale of the movement to recover public spaces in Europe in the 1980s and 1990s. In time, several institutions joined the project, which is presently an initiative of the CCCB working in collaboration with six other European centres: The Architecture Foundation (London), the Architekturzentrum Wien (Vienna), the Cité de l'Architecture et du Patrimoine (Paris), the Nederlands Architectuurinstituut (Rotterdam), the Museum of Finnish Architecture (Helsinki) and the Deutsches Architekturmuseum (Frankfurt). As a result of this joint endeavour, the Prize has become a permanent observatory of European public space.

Besides contemplating the evolution of European cities, the Prize particularly highlights the collective nature and political potential of public spaces. This is the only award of European scope that recognises spaces that are at once public (open and of universal access) and urban. Understanding the power of urban planning to create a political community, the Prize differs from other initiatives that focus on the work, the architect or the landscape by emphasising the relational and civic character of typically urban space. Owing to this political quality, the Prize is awarded to both the author of the work and the developer behind it, who often also guarantees its financing. The Prize then stresses the importance of an alliance between policy and architecture that favours the common good, while recognising representatives from the public sphere who are sensitive to the need for defending public space as an instrument for buttressing democracy. It focuses on examples of urban surgery or those interventions – on the small or large scale – that create community where there was none and that seek to improve the citizens' living conditions. Priority is given, then, to socially sensitive architecture over projects of marked aesthetic accent or spectacular appearance.

Judit Carrera, head of the European Prize for Urban Public Space.

The Prize has an avowed Europe-oriented vocation, which is reflected in its defence of the model of the dense and compact city. Indeed, encouraging debate on the urban nature and even the extent of 'Europe' is one of the CCCB's objectives in offering this Prize. Does a strictly European model of the city exist? What are the limits of Europe? The Prize reaches beyond the bounds of the European Union to take in the greater Europe of the 47 member states of the Council of Europe that have signed the European Convention on Human Rights. Nevertheless, the inclusion of Turkey, Russia or Israel is frequently a matter for discussion (and often a bone of contention) among the jury members, just as it is in European political debate. Whatever the case, in bringing out the shared concerns of the whole continent, the Prize manifests a certain European identity in the spheres of architecture and urban planning.

From its very beginnings, the Prize has created an ideal space for debating, in an ongoing way and with a multidisciplinary focus, some of the central issues of contemporary society, starting out from the city as a universal category. Discussion on the concept of public space, which can be traced back to the origins of philosophy (unity is not the object of the city because the city is pluralism, as Aristotle said), has intensified in recent years as an offshoot of the increasing blurring of the boundaries between the public and the private. This has led some thinkers to call for new concepts such as *collective* space as opposed to the more classical idea of public space. The distinction between the rural and urban domains is also evermore diffuse as is – as a result of this – the frontier between urban planning and landscaping. Over the past ten years, the projects presented for the Prize have reflected the transformation of our urban milieu and the main lines of the debate generated by these changes: matters such as the impact of globalisation on the city, recovery of historic memory, urban peripheries, privatisation and security-oriented management of public spaces and, more recently, the need to uphold formal austerity in architecture, have moved to the forefront of the concerns that European cities have in common. The Prize, like this catalogue, does not eschew the paradoxes that are inherent in the debate on public space in Europe. On the contrary, it gathers them together, discusses them and elaborates them.

These are some of the themes of the in-depth articles to be found in the opening pages of the present catalogue, written by prominent experts associated with the Prize. The director of the CCCB, Josep Ramoneda, opens the reflection herein with an article championing the urban condition of Europe. The architect Manuel de Solà-Morales, president of the 2008 award, criticises the banalisation of the concept of public space and espouses its political nature. Dietmar Steiner, director of Architekturzentrum Wien and a jury member since 2002, relates his particular journey through the history of the Prize. The architect and Pritzker Prize winner, Rafael Moneo, president of the 2010 jury, offers in a hitherto unpublished interview, his definition of the city and public space, along with his analysis of the present situation of architecture. The architect David Bravo, secretary of the 2010 award, draws some theoretical conclusions on the 29 winning projects since 2000. Finally, the architect Elías Torres, president of the 2006 jury, has presented us with a European collage of all the prize-winning works over the past ten years.

In the second part of this catalogue, the 29 projects that won or were given special mention in the first six awards of the Prize are analysed by architects, urban planners, writers, sociologists and political representatives, bringing out, one by one, the common strands of the first decade of the Prize. These works are only a selection of all the projects that can be consulted on-line in the European Archive of Urban Public Space (http://www.publicspace.org). In some cases, ten years have gone by and the works have gained their own autonomy through the citizens' appropriation and the passing of time. In others, the intervention is still recent and their evolution will need to be attentively observed. However, the totality offers a diverse, plural overview of some of the more significant projects from the recent history of public spaces in Europe.

The City and the Human Condition
JOSEP RAMONEDA

1

The city «as place of a particular sort of humanity»: the apophthegm comes from the historian Marc Bloch. The philosopher Claude Lefort takes it up in an essay on Europe as urban civilisation. The argument might be expressed as follows. At the end of the Middle Ages, cities took shape in Europe as places of trade and freedom. Around the market, a nascent social class, the bourgeoisie, gradually gave rise to a new legal order that would end up undermining feudal power. At the same time the serfs, now emancipated from their overlords, found protection in an ever-freer space. Max Weber's formulation centuries later, «city air makes man free» was materialising. In Lefort's words: «The freedom of the city means the dissolution of personal dependence but also the possibility of changing one's condition, favouring work, the capacity of initiative, education and opportunity». For Lefort, this urban community is specific to Europe and explains, in part, its leap forward during the Renaissance. While the European city is a place of trade and freedom, the Chinese city is the territory of bureaucracy and the mandarinate. Hence, Lefort sustains that the political union of Europe, if it is ever completed, will be the product of a secular civilisation of deeply urban character.

2

The European project that arose from the descent into hell, which was the Second World War, was constructed over the taboo of civil war: Europeans would never again kill each other. Yet the countries of Europe are ancient and have too much memory at their backs, and bear too many scars on their bodies inflicted by the weapons of their neighbours. At no time, then, has there been any let-up in the tensions between a singular project of overcoming disagreements in the framework of shared sovereignty and the historic charge of nation states, an invention going back only 200 years that propaganda has striven to make eternal. Nevertheless the project has forged ahead. During the Cold War years, Europe grew as a select club protected by the nuclear umbrella. Later, two new demands appeared along the way: globalisation and the collapse of the Soviet-style regimes. It was no longer just a matter of the political and moral thrust of

Josep Ramoneda, philosopher and director of the Centre of Contemporary Culture of Barcelona.

the beginning of the process; economic need was irrupting onto the scene as well. Globalisation which, more than anything else, is a change of economic scale, was demanding size: only a united Europe could have a voice in the multipolar world of the 21st century. At the same time, it was a duty of democratic Europe to take in those countries that had suffered sequestration under the Soviet communist empire. At last Europe would be whole again: Prague included.

These two new factors have given complexity to the process. The difficulties did not get in the way of achieving a surprising ceding of sovereignty by most of the states: the renunciation of their own legal tenders in favour of a single currency. However, confusion has been growing ever since. The enlargement of Europe is not well digested, the Bush Administration, with the irresponsible complicity of some European leaders, used the East European countries to open up a breach in the continent over the Iraq War and, in the discourse of fatherlands, the crisis has revived the eternal predisposition to endogamous entrenchment in one's home soil. In times of trouble, the temptation to shield oneself behind what is immediately at hand, one's traditional references, is very great. After all, the economy might be globalised but the experience of citizens is fundamentally national and local.

Yet the crisis only adds to the problems. The rejection of the European Constitution by France and Holland put an end to the time of euphemism and ambiguities. What was being whispered finally came to the surface: Europe has a severe democratic deficit. The order of the timing has been right but not the pace. It made sense to build the house from the bottom up: first constructing the economic union so as to enter into political union later. Without the former, the latter was virtually impossible. But incorporation of the citizenry was done too late and badly. People had the sensation of being invited to ratify something that had been cooked up behind their backs. The price to be paid was the Constitution because two countries of democratic tradition wrecked the initiative. Ever since then, a feeling of stagnation and regression has set in, giving a dual impression: mediocrity has taken over the European Union because of a lack of committed leaders. And the nation-states are resisting and trying to keep a firm grip on the process in the midst of great uncertainty.

Cities are open identities as opposed to nations. The seduction of the city arises from the fact that variety is a promise of opportunities.

3

The nation-state was not any old invention. It has been the framework of democracy in Europe. But it has waned in efficiency and, at the same time, is an encumbrance when it comes to bestowing a minimal common identity on Europe. Without a doubt, electing a president through direct universal suffrage would be an important factor working for political integration. But would the president of the French Republic or the king of Spain be prepared to accept a higher-ranking democratic authority?

National culture is a closed unitary culture. It is based on the supposed homogeneity of the citizens that populate the state. Yet this idea of community is totally obsolete today in societies that, in their composition, can no longer conceal their heterogeneity. Is it time to go back to this «place of a particular sort of humanity» that is the European city? Cities are open identities as opposed to nations, which are closed identities. Might they constitute adequate nodes for weaving together a network of basic European identification? Cities, says Zygmunt Bauman, are about «sharing space with strangers, living in the unsolicited yet obtrusive proximity of strangers». The seduction of the city arises from the fact that variety is a promise of opportunities.

The city is the place where the majority of European citizens live. Cities have certainly become, to use Bauman's words, «... *dumping grounds for globally begotten problems*» [Bauman's italics]. The spectre of uncertainty generated by globalisation and the ideology of fear threatens the city with fracture. There are cities in the world where the different social sectors live cloistered away, separated by walls and barriers with hardly any contact between them. 'Urbanalisation', to use Francesc Muñoz's coinage, the divorce of *urbs* and *civitas* (Françoise Choay) by means of indiscriminate occupation of territory by disperse urbanisation in the form of thousands upon thousands of duplexes and their gardens, is threatening the dense city, territory of anonymity and freedom. However, in spite of everything, Europe has managed to maintain the intensity of its cities. And it has had to take on the conflicts and, inasmuch as it is possible, turn them into factors of opportunity. After all, what has sustained the particular way of being of European cities has been the welfare state and this will be on the European scale or it will not exist.

4

It is in cities where changes take place. It is in cities where it is still possible for public space to work as a place of meeting and contact, indispensable for mutual recognition, which is the basis for any form of truly possible coexistence. Cities are what comprise the connecting nodes. Europe will soon have inscribed in its geography a mesh of high-speed trains with the great cities at its vertices. Mobility is an essential factor in European construction which, in this domain, lags a long way behind the United States.

The city is, above all, the place of open identity, the place wherein it is possible to find a common denominator among the strangers who comprise it. This is a minimum identity very similar to that required for the construction of a European consciousness. An identity based on recognition of the other and in defence of a European model that has all the elements of an urban culture: sovereignty shared among strangers; political solidarity; diversity and conflict as bearers of opportunities and change; and negotiation and dialogue as ways of relating. Without any need to genuflect before any lesser god, whether it is the fatherland or the religion of the day.

5

At this point, the urban question is faced with a basic problem arising from globalisation: the human condition. I would venture to say that, today, the human condition is the urban condition.

What leads us to rethink the human condition? The most important phenomenon of the 20th century is related with population. In spite of being the century in which humans have killed each other more than ever before, with four genocides and an endless series of cruel wars, humanity has more than doubled its life expectancy and the number of the planet's inhabitants has quadrupled. It took all the time from prehistory through to the end of the 19th century to double human life expectancy. Now, this feat – if it might be called such – has been achieved in 100 years. This exponential increase in population has brought about a massive displacement of human beings from the countryside to the city. The city, place of the freedom of anonymity, has become the receptacle for all the problems of the world. Yet the city is the place where human beings will decide their immediate future. The population increase, combined with the technological revolution that has ushered in this change of scale we call globalisation, has demolished the old myth of homogenous societies constructed around the nation-state, which was the

> *It is in cities where it is still possible for public space to work as a place of meeting and contact, indispensable for mutual recognition, which is the basis for any form of truly possible coexistence.*

product of the expulsion and exclusion of all kinds of minorities that disturbed the appearance of basic cultural unity.

All the processes of globalisation known to humanity – the conquest of America, for example, or the different imperialisms of the 19th century – have swallowed up institutions and cultures, sowing doubts about the human condition along the way. It was father Francisco de Vitoria who made it clear that the Indians were children of God, just as racism was part and parcel of the modern imperialisms that entertained European citizens with fairs and freak-shows where human beings from the colonies were put on display as if they were exotic animals.

Once again, given the imperative need for different peoples to learn to live together, it now behoves us to repeat the question about the human condition. And the answer to the question bears within it the cosmopolitan question – a single species, a possible truth, a minimal shared morality – and the urban question – the place of the experience of living among strangers.

6

Is there a human condition that is shared by the thousands of millions of inhabitants of the world, with the cosmopolitan complement that the idea of humanity entails? Or was Nietzsche right in believing we are approaching the fracture of humanity between the 'last man' (*der letzte Mensch*) and the 'superman' (*Übermensch*)? Man is at once an autonomous being and a relational being: his dignity resides in thinking and deciding for himself while he also grows and is shaped by participating in social life. The human being alone is nothing: she is forged in relation with the rest. At the same time, it is in her autonomy that she attains the plenitude of a being that stands for freedom. Thinking (reason) and deciding (freedom) are two attributes that distinguish the human being from other living beings. Herein lies the crux of the story that seeks a universal common denominator. The fact that every story has its own singularities and peculiarities does not exclude the human condition from being pondered as a whole.

The great demographic leap has meant that the city has become the place where contemporary human experience belongs. Learning to experience different people is the opposite of what the classical nation-state proposed for its pretension of homogeneity, which was constructed over ejection, denial and oblivion. Moors, Moriscos and Jews were expelled from Spain and, for all that, it was still not possible to achieve the complete closure of a unitary state. The city is the opposite of closed identity discourse. Hence the nation-states of Europe are presently an obstacle, a restraint on the processes of transfer of power to a world that calls for shared sovereignty between the supranational and the local and a progressive fading away of the national.

7

Human rights have been the minimum common denominator of the human condition with which the modern process has identified. It is evident that the conversion of the human rights doctrine into a weapon by means of which one part of humanity – so-called western civilisation – has set about the conquest of the other part has disfigured their role and still more so when attempts have been made to impose them through the devastation of war or torture. The postcolonial countries are right when they say that human rights haven't reached them yet or, if they have, they are completely mutilated. The human condition is rather more than a few shared rights. And the chance of rethinking it clashes with two concepts in use with which the West prolongs its incapacity for empathy with any cosmopolitanism worthy of the name: the concept of civilisation and the theoretical and practical disaster that multiculturalism has turned out to be. Both commit the same error: claiming that man bears his identity like a brand, from the day of his birth. For the concept of civilisation, the pivotal factor of human identity is religion, which definitively determines us while, for multiculturalism, it is cultural origin. From free subjects who grow in the experience of diversity we turn into beings enslaved by roots that cannot be renounced. This is the same old story on which nation-states conceived in terms of fixed frontiers fed and flourished but which happens to be obsolete in a world that inevitably tends to ever-variable borders. Is there any other place of change that can beat the city's capacity for mutation?

The city has become the place where contemporary human experience belongs.

8

The city as a place of political articulation, which is to say as a territory of conflict between human beings capable of thinking and deciding, and emancipated from the decisive trappings of the organic. A polyvalent being, able to combine multiple identities. The human condition as urban condition. The human question is the question of recognition: recognising each other, recognising the other and bestowing on him or her the right to be recognised (Axel Honneth).

Rethinking the human condition, then, means going back over the forms of denial of recognition that populate our everyday settings.

The suicide terrorist, who puts into question everything we might call the minimum protocol of communication among human beings: neither you nor I want to die. The breaking of this convention gives rise to utter bewilderment. The suicide terrorist takes his or her nihilist impulse to its ultimate expression: fulfilment in death, killing the other and oneself. This is what heightens the feeling of horror. As Jacqueline Rose has written, the bafflement comes from the «unbearable intimacy shared in their final moments by the suicide bomber and her or his victims. Suicide bombing is an act of passionate identification – you take the enemy with you in a deadly embrace». How can you believe in your own humanity if you don't believe in that of the enemy? Is there some tragic recognition of the other in dragging him or her with you in the most absolute nihilist consumption?

The *illegal*.[1] Human beings without rights who move amongst us. Human beings who are denied the most elementary recognition. Since the Berlin Wall came down the world has been broken up by a proliferation of walls. The Berlin Wall prevented people from leaving while, in their majority, today's walls prevent people from coming in. In particular, they send out a dreadful message to an immense part of humanity: to get here you pay the toll of death. The border fences of Ceuta and Melilla suffice to serve as an example.

The person who is unequipped for production. Technological change has wrought a double rupture that feeds back into itself: the growth of inequalities and electronic illiteracy. The issue of equality has been fading out of political and ideological debate, and has become a nuisance for the left as well. Yet, here, there is a very serious risk of species fracture. Recently, when mobs in South Africa set upon

---

1. The adjective *ilegal*, as applied to undocumented immigrants, is frequently used in Spanish in adjectival form alone, without a substantive as if, even in grammar, material – human – existence is being denied to these human beings [translator].

immigrants coming from surrounding countries, Achille Mbembe described the problem at the root of it all: in a country like South Africa that, thanks to apartheid, has accumulated a huge educational backwardness, there are millions of people who cannot find a useful place in the productive system. Work as a central factor of recognition is an element common to all ideologies, with the single exception of some kinds of anarchism.

The fundamentalist, which is the name used to signal the bearer of a closed identity, one in which the factors of religion and fatherland are determinant. The fundamentalist is always the other: this deceit must be taken apart. Attention must be given to the new fundamentalisms, camouflaged under the technocratic face.

The sexist: he who uses gender as a form of discrimination. As Daniel Innerarity points out, that day that males recognise that they also have gender, things might change.

The tax-identification-number citizen who comes out of a culture that directly produces the subject as being at once subject and object of consumption: competitor, consumer and taxpayer. Everything is consumed – the human subject as well.

9

With all this resistance to recognition, the risk of totalitarianism of indifference keeps rising. This is perhaps what Alain Touraine calls the disappearance of society. The triumph of money as bearer of normative capacity. In the developed world the flame of social irritation is flickering out, politics is just one more consumer item and the politician an object of consumption, of whom almost everything is demanded. The space of the possible is shrinking. This is not so much about the identity storm and the return of the religious as about an increasing loss of political space: global economic power, national and local political power, experience of the national and local citizen. Could the city be the place of political articulation and social restructuring? Or are we entering a phase of history in which man renounces being of flesh and blood and Internet space takes over the imaginary and the economy of desire until becoming the only possible space in which to think about the politics of the future?

Are we heading for being a species that is a stranger to itself? The city is the place in which the human condition must be capable of self-recognition. Yet the city is not exactly enjoying its heyday since it is submitted to the pressures of 'urbanalisation', of rampant speculation and exclusion in the form of peripheries. There is an urgent need to repair enlightened critical reason, correcting its main, dual error:

Public space is the place of conflict and conflicts aren't resolved but they metamorphose and are transformed. The desire for definitive resolution means war, is totalitarianism.

denial of the complexity of the economy of desire and overconfidence in the power of good. Evil is abuse of power. Reaction against flagrant injustice has to be the driving force behind the construction of minimal politics and minimal morality, as Amartya Sen suggests in his *The Idea of Justice*. Evaluation of conflict is a contribution of modern democracy. Speaking of its social aspect, Marx proclaimed the overcoming of conflict. Speaking of inner conflict, Freud proposed a rebalancing that would make it possible to come to grips with conflict. The debate continues along these lines. Public space is the place of conflict and conflicts aren't resolved but they metamorphose and are transformed. The desire for definitive resolution means war, is totalitarianism. Hence, the city (from Troy or from Sodom and Gomorrah to Sarajevo) has been razed, destroyed so many times throughout history. And with it, the human condition.

The Impossible Project of Public Space

MANUEL DE SOLÀ-MORALES

A deliberation such as this is confronted with a terminological problem: the semantic debasement of the term 'public space', which is indiscriminately used for any exercise in land-filling, transforming or prettifying vacant land. All too often, the category of 'public space' is used without taking into account the requirement of real urban quality that the term entails. This urbanity is the quality of significant places of collective and political content in their very material form. 'Material urbanity', the ability of urban material to express civic, aesthetic, functional and social meanings, is a basic concept when it comes to defining public space and, hence, intrinsic to the aims of this Prize.

Otherwise, a cramming of forms and planimetric geometries, the unease of frustrated architectural projects at zero elevation, or an arbitrary compositional interplay of surfaces can come to occupy public terrains with apparently infinite freedom. Mannerism is conspicuous, while the vocabulary of alignments, lamp posts, pavements, high ground and low ground, pergolas, ramps and green patches burgeons *ad nauseam*.

The pervasive magnitude of such practices, the growing number of projects (whether in squares and streets, parks, service installations and facilities or other places) would seem to make it necessary to re-propose a strict notion of public space as a material condition (locus) of political space.

Civic space is very difficult. Some projects merely reform outmoded spaces which are, on occasion, of great urban significance, to give them innovative or surprising, subjectively affirmative forms. Others confront new spheres of urban growth in order to procure therein some expression of public dignity. Still others understand the site as an available empty area, making the most of the occasion to invent new artifices, installations of a new urban symbology.

Yet, whatever the case and for all these limitations, there appears the indisputable fact of the high average quality attained in different municipalities by the methodological effort and technological trainning of the professionals concerned, the growing attention of public authorities and the great degree of satisfaction among the citizens with these projects. This is an extraordinary process of the invention, over 20 years, of a socially and culturally recognised quasi-discipline.

Manuel de Solà-Morales, architect, director of Laboratori d'Urbanisme, Barcelona.

Material urbanity, the ability of urban material to express civic, aesthetic, functional and social meanings, is a basic concept when it comes to defining public space and, hence, intrinsic to the aims of this Prize.

Speaking of public space can be a rhetorical convention that covers up the confusion that stands out over and above the values pertaining to the city as a political place, place of subjective interaction, place of the 'polis'. If we accept the hypothesis (advanced since 1992) that it is the *collective* condition that defines urbanity and that, therefore, the collectivisation of spaces and homes, people and institutions, economic movements and activities, is the supreme effect entailed by urbanity, then we would have to think that all the places of the city, public and private, individual or corporative, are partly public spaces since they share the way in which they are appropriate for the citizens. The buildings and streets of a city, the squares and monuments, factories and schools are, in good part, felt as belonging to the residents and, to the extent that they are affected by their functional and aesthetic characteristics, they are the object of citizens' opinions and claims. In contrast, a rural cultivation or construction is free of this collective dependence: it is an autonomous fact, isolated in its internal logic and does not form part of any formal integrated collective but, rather, belongs to the collective that is simply referred to in neighbourhood relations (or the superstructural notion of 'landscape' as an environmental value, without express political content).

Hence, if all urban space is more or less public (and all public space is more or less of or for private interests), what would be the specificity of what we conventionally call 'public spaces'? What would a Prize (European or otherwise) for 'public space' projects be about? Can we determine which projects count and which ones don't as such spaces? And once they are singled out, should the projects be evaluated for the intensity in which they are 'public' (the more 'public' a project, the higher the grade), or according to how good the spaces are (more attractive, more functional, more impressive), or for the degree to which they incorporate certain critical questions that the contemporary city has not yet managed to collectivise (traffic, segregation, largeness of scale, sustainability)?

These are questions that are interesting not only for jury members since they also rebound on the definition itself, questioning the specific nature of public space and maximally so when the deliberation is not so much about real public spaces but about 'projects' of would-be real spaces. Does this, then, belong to the jurisdiction of inventiveness, design or innovation? Is it formal surprise or thematic modernity that has greater value? Is it difficulty overcome or is it effectiveness of transformation?

To go still further, what is it that constitutes public space as real experience? Over and above sociological, political and functional reflections, what has just made public space recognisable is a material fact. A fact where aesthetics is frequently distorted and distorting, yet where expression and communication pass through a particular material configuration.

The great amount of work carried out in recent years on public spaces, the mushrooming of assignments and projects, the tireless energy of architects and engineers, designers and artists, landscapers and botanists – all of them set on enhancing scraps of non-built-up urban land – the ideological discussion and the intellectual strivings towards bestowing a theoretical status and/or disciplinary entity to these matters, have extraordinarily enriched professional practices and heightened the attention of public administrators. Interest in public space seems to be self-justifying. And this, if exaggerated, can lead to unintended results. Not only words can lose their sense but the works themselves can too. The number of interventions, the arbitrariness of the projects, the frequency in space and time, the copying of cliché models and figures, the fashions and squandering of economic resources can pervert the original nature of public space as collective space *par excellence*: space that is not appropriated for any fad, or author or actor, or any currently prominent politician, a place that is available for open interpretation and an intersection of interests.

Public space or showroom? The very valuable collection of projects that the CCCB has been putting together over the years, as with the European Archive for Urban Public Space, can simultaneously give rise to contradictory feelings of admiration and misgiving. This is a catalogue of excellence that permits one to discover what terms – old and new – have captured the attention of administrators and project designers, and what examples have been giving rise to prototypes and sequences. It is an incontrovertible demonstration of the enormous surge in attention to matters pertaining to the city's public affairs and the public cost-effectiveness of giving them material form in different corners of the city or in available bits of land. Again, however, the sight of so many projects all together also lays bare the

Public space as a combined structure of different streets and squares is the essence, the substance of coexistence, interaction and the redundancy that shared life brings.

repetition of a lot of gratuitous gesturing and a great deal of gymnastics in forms striving for originality and surprise, as if public land were a blank page for the personal pleasure of the project designer. Undulations, ruptures, continuities and rows, screens and splodges, are combined – always out of the blue – as pieces of a closed and self-referencing composition.

It would appear that the proliferation of these sorts of jobs is tending to bring about a new form of autonomous professional practice which sees the precinct where the work is to be done as a free range in which zero-elevation architecture might be invented, an unconstrained exercise in which – relatively – low-cost forms and images can be explored in freedom that could not exist in construction that is constantly submitted to the much stricter requirements of the programme, costs, functions, structure and client.

In dealing with public space, one finds that it may be the leading issue of urban form or it can be mere anecdote. It depends on the scale (not the measure) in which we look at it. Public space as a combined structure of different streets and squares is the essence, the substance of coexistence, interaction and the redundancy that shared life brings. Designing the structure of spaces for the mobility, leisure and representation that link spaces of activity is what traditional urban planning is all about. In a certain sense, thinking that the quality and form of shared spaces is prior to and more important than pinpointing particular functions is now a methodological option that is rarely taken.

Yet it is not the scale of the urban whole that we usually have in mind when we speak of 'public spaces'. To the extent that we keep circumscribing the idea of public space to a precise, delimited place, we are losing our perspective on it as a basic urban structure and giving priority instead to the singularity – morphological or environmental – of each site as an autonomous urban lot, as an occasion for independent formalisation. Hence, the many commissions for designing large or small public spaces viewed as specific objects turn into drawings of a closed lot, self-referencing designs frequently with an arbitrary perimeter. The site is thus converted into a platform of experimentation, a showroom in which to play with paving and lamp posts, slopes and corners, with the utmost independence.

Again, the extension of this plethora of project-designing activity covers a considerable range of countries and cities. The interest in breathing modernity into public land is expressed in the demand everywhere and each project, each civic example, can be understood, from a certain standpoint, as part of an extensive process that, over the past 20 years, has been bringing about a wide-ranging renovation of the whole urban epidermis of Europe. As in the periodical cellular replacement of human skin, the connective surface of European cities, their interstitial tissue of roads and paths, of gardens and squares, of what is most common or substantial and also most structural and most necessary of urban space, is being replaced, extended and manifested. What, thanks to its basic condition, was once taken as being obvious – paving, offering stable physical support for the contact of urban things and the mobility of citizens – is now an optional and symbolic matter, a question of design.

The construction of public land, hitherto the immediate result of technical needs and means, is nowadays the object of alternative offers and questionable taste. An aerial view of the map of Europe with coloured lights illuminating the progressive work over the paved surface of Europe would impress us with its extension and variety. And it is difficult to overstate the importance of this vision. This is a historic step in the concept of the city, as space held in common, in the idea of public space as a material place.

Perhaps it will only be after this careful, overall urban planning momentum, this process of expansive culturalisation of the European ground-plan, that the merits of the different projects might be judged, for what they manage to establish as a general idea of urban space and not only as attractive planimetric gestuality.

After all, at bottom, almost all the projects are works of repaving, more or less initiatives of replacing the urban skin, a surface that is in itself a deep structure. Paving, with ground as support and link, has an extensive and not a singular condition and proclaims the central role of interdependence. Public spaces will be just that when they construct the combined system of urban space and not merely a closed work. When they are defining elements of a model of the city without perimeters, rather than zero-elevation architecture. When they become the representation of mobility, coexistence and conflict rather than stylised, neatly resolved landscape.

Scrutiny of the projects present in the European Archive for Urban Public Space suggested to me that they should be sorted according to their stance as proposals and their methodological pretensions. It is not easy, I believe, to produce the usual typological, thematic or scale-oriented classifications. The precise intention behind the project, which is not easy to divine either, can help us, however, to advance in critical knowledge of public space practice. Four types may be distinguished here:

This is a historic step in the concept of the city, as space held in common, in the idea of public space as a material place.

1 Tidying-up projects. There are many projects (the greater part) that re-order spaces on top of themselves, making them more useful, more attractive and more novel. They respond to political intentions of visible investment, which are specific to more difficult or more representative spaces. They set out to bring them up to date and spruce them up.
Rarely do these projects convey any content other than a good makeup job.
The evaluation to be made in this case is primarily functional.

2 Projects that expand the previous sphere of public space and that, even while sticking to known typological guidelines, set about designing new areas, different in scale and location, either because of topographical difficulties or thematic complexity. This is basic urban planning activity.
These works have a technical value.

3 Projects that collectivise. These projects, the most incisive, accept the strategic goal of creating public space with private ingredients, on the basis of an understanding of collective space (public+private) as a defining substance of what is urban. Explicitly or otherwise, such projects take the view that urbanising means collectivising, and they may have a lot or a little in terms of form, but they do not shape. Rather, they are actions of mental strategy. In their intimate sense, they have a political value.

4 Projects that invent. These are the few initiatives that are born of an ill-defined occasion, without any specific programme, without purpose and without clear limits. They propose uncommon images on the basis of inventing a type of public space for which, precisely, there is no type. It is the invention of form and programme at the same time and means accepting the risk – of error, or failure – as a premise of planning.
The value here is artistic.

However, it is also necessary to stipulate that not all public space entails urban quality just because it has been successfully organised. A project can value the characteristics of the place and can express landscaping or utilitarian qualities without managing to give material form to any notion of urbanity. The rehabilitation of the Gavà beaches near Barcelona, for example, has produced an excellent, sensitive and intelligent public leisure space but it does not express the urban quality that, in contrast, is to be found in the Mar Bella shoreline project, also in Barcelona, which is perhaps less attractive. The aims and contact with urban complexity are so different in these two cases that, whatever their intrinsic merits, we cannot consider the former as urban space while the latter can come under that heading. We might say much the same if we compare the Plaça Europa and the Plaça Lesseps in Barcelona. The infrastructural density and formalist vocation of the former cannot contribute urban quality to the site because of the devastating effect of the design materials, the measurements, forms and elements while, in contrast, the chaotic solutions in the Plaça Lesseps are surpassed as a whole by the active and heterogeneous centrality of the place and the permissive tolerance of all the lateral manifestations (of facades, movements, angles of vision and uneven surfaces) that have appeared.

Neither can the ring routes, as intrinsically circulatory spaces, be regarded as urban space. The evident absence of any relationship with the adjoining city and the highly homogeneous character of their support materials, reduce any urban quality to mere mechanical channels. This is the case despite the 'urbanising' efforts that have so meritoriously been attempted. In fact, this is an act of oversimplifying urban complexity, reducing it to monographic landscape. The subway, on the other hand, is usually a 'hyper-urban' space: the parts we see and understand (entrances and stations) are made up of people, signs, connections and train carriages, all of them different materials that suggest a high degree of urban quality. What we do not see – the tunnels – are black and make of the mechanical part of transport an absent, irrelevant fact.

All public space projects are precisely that in the sense of public conception and administration. But not all of them constitute spaces of urbanity in the civic, political and figurative senses that go with the good city. Some are spaces for the public and others are urban public spaces. Public space combines 'urban things', physical materials that are able to make perceptible an idea of the city. Hegel said that beauty is the perceptible expression of an idea. And this is the grandeur and difficulty of public spaces. Ground and mud, cobblestones and slabs, asphalt and concrete, wood and leaves on the trees shift here from being generic to compo-

All public space projects are precisely that in the sense of public conception and administration. But not all of them constitute spaces of urbanity in the civic, political and figurative senses that go with the good city.

nents for making urban quality a material thing. Walls, land, lamp posts, doorways, ramps, vehicles, corners and crannies establish the sensations of the mind that bring people into relation.

The city, macle of conflict and solidarity, stability and dynamism, connection and distance, appears in the material condition of public space. Over and above sociological, political and functional considerations, public space imposes itself as a material fact, a substratum joining matter and idea, trying to ensure that it turns out to be beautiful. Walter Benjamin, Richard Sennett, Paul Virilio and Fredric Jameson have given much thought to all this.

Physical urban quality is in the measure, the proper understanding of the limits of a space. As soon as we define it, we segregate it. Good public space has no limits, or the ones it has are undefined, multiple, oscillating. As a relative place, its references to the urban whole are more important than its own identity and yet this is enhanced thanks to them. Watch those perimeters! They are both main theme and baptism of fire of urban quality.

The urban nature of urban materials also lies in the sense of touch. Even more than in sight, perhaps. In public space, personal experience, the route and comfort are fundamental. Walking on a hard or soft surface, stone or sand, on corrugated or slippery ground brings about very different sorts of contact between body and brain. The idea is transmitted through the different sensations of the material used. And the proximity of the hands to railings, walls and benches makes us experience, more than in any other sense, the character of space. If by means of sight we understand shaping, size and setting, by touch we experience identity, treatment and character.

In the contemporary city, we can no longer see public spaces with reference to a notion of urban, functional or semantic structure, as we did in the years of structuralism but, like the Greeks, we need to read civilised space as a topological, tactical order. We must go beyond landscaping decorativeness and recognise the warp and weft of materials, which is what the proto-modern Gottfried Semper studied and called for.

In the thinking of the 1970s and the following years, little was said about public space except, perhaps, the notion of centrality as the symbolic locus of life in common. Henri Lefebvre, who showed great foresight at the time, criticised the city of the Modern Movement, saying that '*la ville est du trans-fonctionnel durable*', already seeking rupture in the paradigm of structure as the idea of a city. Today, perhaps, leaving aside all the many tricky metaphors used as an excuse for a project, one must seek instead an idea (of public space, of a bit of city, of urban quality, of a political place) in the absence, precisely, of symbolic images, or picturesque novelty (all, alas, globalised) and a possibility of civic identity in the dissolution of the individual place in the collective milieu, in pure citizenship.

The individual is attenuated when public space is offered as a readied room. Napoleon, when he reached the Piazza San Marco on invading Venice, said that it is «the most beautiful salon in Europe», seeing in it a space to be used in keeping with norms and customs; the exact opposite of Barcelona residents freely enjoying Mar Bella. Desacralised public space is the condition for the city's existence and without public space the only things left are the rural setting and castles.

Interview with Rafael Moneo
MAGDA ANGLÈS / JUDIT CARRERA

A week after the winners of the European Prize for Urban Public Space 2010 were announced, we visited Rafael Moneo at his studio in a two-storey house in the El Viso district of Madrid. Surrounded by a small garden, the building, an example of early 20th-century Madrid-style rationalist architecture and at ease with its chipped façade, bears the sheen of distinction endowed by the passing of time. We make ourselves comfortable in a cosy living room in which piles of books on architecture are scattered around tables, chairs and floor. Rafael Moneo describes for us his experience as president of the 2010 jury and talks about his particular perspective on the city and contemporary architecture as he sketches on a piece of tracing paper.

How would you evaluate the results of the European Prize for Urban Public Space 2010?

This award constitutes an index of what is understood by public space, both for architects and for the general public. It is an indicator, a witness, a sample of what it means at a particular time in urban-planning thinking and in the present-day situation of architecture and urban design. The fact of having awarded the Prize *ex aequo* to two projects like the Magdeburg Library in Germany and the Oslo Opera House in Norway is something natural and no arbitrary choice. This point has a certain interest.

The Magdeburg Library reveals its goals very directly: the users themselves are very keen to strip buildings of their monumental condition and directly claim their values in terms of use, values that generically contribute towards underpinning the notion of virtue that goes hand-in-hand with culture. With a minimal intervention one is made aware of the essential role of urban design. Moreover, it embraces the desire to recycle and stylistically speaking, too, this has turned out to be an unprejudiced building. It shows a certain lack of interest in strictly formal inquiry and architectural investigation and yet it is open to other cultural aspects of wider scope, whether it is in its contents or through its recycling of all these features of 1950s architecture. Here, inadvertently, there is a polemical assumption of the political language of the 1950s as an alternative to the more exhibitionist and exuberant architectural language of the 1990s and the first decade of this century. Again, one finds the reformist volition of a small community in its wish to transform a road junction into something that has urban life.

Rafael Moneo, architect and Josep Lluís Sert Professor in the Department of Architecture of the Graduate School of Design, Harvard University.

This is a highly interesting project and it is not in contradiction with the other *ex aequo* winner, the Oslo Opera House, one of the most significant buildings of recent years and of greatest intellectual ambition in being such a high-ranking building in such a mature country and, moreover, one with so many means available. With this project Snøhetta presents something that is very characteristic of architecture today. The Oslo Opera House is a really symptomatic example of the desire that presently prompts architects to make architecture dissolve and become landscape. There is something of this in the proposals of all these people who understand landscape, gardens and parks as public space. Located in a place that is as urban as the port of Oslo, where there are also buildings like the City Hall, and with such a will and such desire to express and materialise what a city is, this project strives to shed the most distinctive features of buildings in order to dissolve into the natural setting. The ramps of the Opera House, for example, end up dropping into the sea so that they are transformed into elements that are almost natural scenery: the building aspires to be topography. Yet when the visitor goes inside to see what the building is about, he or she discovers an opera theatre in the purely traditional Italian style. Here we have the flagrant contradiction between something that comes out of urban life, for example an opera house, and a recipient – a work of architecture – that wants to be landscape. This kind of imposition inevitably occurs. The jury recognised this value and intrinsic difficulty.

How might one explain this adulteration of architecture by landscape?

I believe that this is basically the result of two factors. The first we should mention is a deliberate confrontation with the architecture of the previous generation which, like it or not, is understood nowadays as exaggeratedly monumental. If we accept that the works of Frank Gehry and the bold architecture of Rem Koolhaas dominated the architecture of the 1980s and 1990s, we'll confirm that they've had no problem in getting into the monumental dimension by way of hyperbole. The second reason, which might be the more influential one here, is the desire to bring architecture close to nature which, in keeping with the dominant ideology, might be described as ecological. Today's architects are less interested in pursuing a city under the sway of bourgeois discretion – the 19th-century city, the one that Aldo Rossi liked – one that observes the rules and, yes, a city in which nature, the ecological dimension is present. Garden cities aspired to nature as a goal when the new means of transport enabled city-dwellers to recover the nature revealed by the English landscapers. The garden city satisfied the ideals of people who be-

> *One cannot think that any figure is completely closed, that any city has attained its plenitude.*

lieved that social life and the natural environment didn't have to be understood as opposites. Nevertheless, critics of the garden city soon appeared. Le Corbusier argued that the garden city is a complete waste. The fact is that this present return to nature of architecture that purports to be ecological totally disregards the garden city. The proposals of the ecological architecture that is produced for us today abound in visual aspects, enveloping its constructions in green. Architecture vanishes beneath an artificial mantle of plants, the efficiency and cost of which should be called into question. However this ecological pitch has become a cliché and, accordingly, architecture now seems to want to dissolve into the landscape. A critique of the kinds of architecture that presently claim to be ecological and sustainable is yet to be done. In the real world, genuinely ecological responses need to be sought in primitive architecture. One must recognise that a lot of ancient architecture has been equally or more ecological than today's, despite the efforts architects make nowadays to emulate it. I don't mean by this that there should be a return to vernacular architecture, but it should be recognised that rationality is more present and more evident in the primitive. Rationality is reflected in the form of what is constructed. To some extent, the fewer the means available, the more rationality appears in the constructive response. Today there is such a profusion of means that the builder sets about the job apparently without limitations. This leads to the notion that anything is constructible, to a new concept that seems to accept as legitimate anything that can be constructed. One should be talking about *buildability* as the only limit to the architect's imagination. Naturally, this standpoint that is so rife today bears little relation with the rationality that ought to be implicit to true ecological architecture.

In some of your writings you've spoken of the importance of *place* in earlier times, contextualisation or the «murmur of the site». Do you think that this notion is on the way out?

I believe in the site. One fears that the new cities, such as those in the Persian Gulf, lack this support that, at a certain point, ensures that cities are bound up with geography, that each city finds its sense through its location. I very much fear that they are no more than the expression of financial operations since they are occupied by the people who are constructing them and are nothing but commodities bought up by investors who may never occupy them. This lack of interest in context unquestionably leaves architecture without the incentives that site bestows and that are so important when it comes to imagining what is constructed. What I've just remarked might be extended to the materials that stimulate the mind of the person who's going to construct. We're talking about a time in which the versatility of techniques and the possibility of constructing almost anything mean that the builder does not understand or apply the positive limitations that used to exist in the proper use of a particular material. The concept of form was once intimately linked to materials and techniques of construction and, at bottom, the architect found in such limitations the starting point and sustenance of his or her formal fantasies. Somebody who constructed in stone faced certain limits and obligations, the definition of form: the reasons for constructing were implicit in the material. Today, form is approached without these restraints and limitations. The facilities offered now by the figurative worlds represented by the computer, without this filter of constructive knowledge, mean that new builders find that they have less underpinning.

It might be said that one only constructs over the constructed. Constructing over the constructed always provides clues, permits contrasts to be established and makes it possible to testify to the value of what one thinks, which doesn't happen when the work can be produced autonomously and independently. Rarely does an autonomous and independent work happen without some limitations. Again, it is more beautiful to think that one is working on an unfinished building and contributing to an endless job, which is the construction of the planet at any given time. Our task is always linked up with something bigger. It is beautiful to think of the history of cities in this way. Seen from this point of view, the city has less to do with the city imagined from utopian thinking. I like to see the city as a building on which we are all working but one that we shall never see completed. One cannot think that any figure is completely closed, that any city has attained its plenitude.

The beautiful thing about the architect's endeavour is the ability to divest oneself totally of one's work. The architect transfers to the building an instrumental condition, one of use. At times people tend to think that this happens with all kinds of work or artistic production. Does the same thing happen with a poem? I'm not sure. It's true that a poem doesn't end in the concepts brought together on the page and also that it is multiplied with the readers, but it doesn't happen in the same way. The bonds that join the building and the architect are weaker than those between poem and author. I believe that the grandeur of architecture lies in its ability to bestow life – its own life – on what is being constructed. I don't know if

A city is perhaps one of the most complete materialisations of the life of men and history. Few manifestations so completely include time and present, the throb of life.

this happens with a poem and think, in any case, that it is less so with a painting. The idea of the reader as owner of the text is a half truth. However, inasmuch as the building, and not the architect, is owner of itself, the person who uses it takes possession of it, makes it his or hers in a more natural way. The architectural work is associated with the architect but buildings have their own life and establish a direct, immediate relationship with their users. It is only relatively speaking that an architect is owner of the building.

The notion of public space has traditionally been associated with the idea of democracy. To what point does physical proximity between strangers in the city generate political community?

I've just got back from the capital of Peru and the phenomenon of Lima is that of shantytown construction. It's a really interesting city whose population has multiplied by ten over the last decades. When Mario Vargas Llosa wrote *The City and the Dogs* and *Conversation in the Cathedral* Lima possibly had some six or eight hundred thousand inhabitants. Today there are ten or 15 times as many. Country people come to the city wanting another way of life and the extremely modest do-it-yourself construction they are immediately engaged in means that the city is understood as physical proximity. Lima's shantytowns are city: the people who live in them believe they are constructing the city, and indeed they are. There is a whole tradition in this kind of construction but it doesn't mean that there are unwritten rules to be respected, or that there is a certain notion of order. The other way of making a city is constructing infrastructure. This is not the case in Lima where what I think the essential thing to recognise is that it is the physical proximity of people that gives sense to the setting wherein architecture intervenes, and this immediately becomes city. People who live in the shantytowns of Lima don't see proximity as a problem for living in community. On the contrary, they understand it as what they seek and what they value most.

The classical link between physical space and democracy is related with the awareness that it is in life with others – and only on the basis of life with others – that we may understand our passage through this world. The city is the framework for this life in common and this life in common is what leads to these aspects of specialisation in the city that ends up being understood as a set of buildings reflecting different tasks, whether we're talking about a school, a theatre or a market. Giving to the word 'market' this connotation, whereby everything that one would like to do, acquire or possess is accessible, is a good way of understanding the city. I think it was Max Weber who understood the city as a market, but I've often had the occasion to quote the words of Louis Kahn who says that the city is the place where a child learns, or can learn, what he or she wants to be. I agree because it is linked up with this idea of market and also of professions, ways of life, how one would like to be in this world, in what profession to devote one's time, and all this can only be learned in contact with others. This is why I'm loath to think about a virtual, disperse city, without contact with other people.

Unfortunately, the modern city is seeing a decline in the diversity of possible vocations. In the end you don't know if this city that Louis Kahn was speaking of, where there were carpenters, upholsterers, ironmongers, shopkeepers, day labourers, scribes, and all the trades, has anything to do with the city today. Yet this is the city for which we feel nostalgia. And this explains why we feel so good in old cities that conserve the memory of a city, like a Noah's Ark of the professions. Sad to say, today's city often has to be seen as a mere theme park.

Tourism is a very destructive thing. All the mayors who want to turn their cities into tourist places don't know that the greatest luxury a city can enjoy is not to have tourists. Barcelona is still big enough to resist being destroyed by tourism since it is concentrated in certain neighbourhoods but there are many small cities that are consumed by tourism, and one might mention Florence, Venice or Rome itself. At bottom is globalisation, along with the ease with which we move around and enjoy other cities. It's true that our pleasure in different worlds comes at the price of admitting that they don't belong to us and this fact of not belonging will always mean that, with other cities, we can only experience them as foreign, distant worlds. I think that the city experienced only with the tempo of tourism is hard to understand as a city. I don't know if we're talking about the same relationship that one can have with a book. And it's not because one can read the city like a book but because there comes a time in which one enjoys the condition of the city, its plenitude, in a way that is not so very different from the way one takes pleasure in the integrity of a book or the synoptic view of a painting. A city is enjoyed; I'm not saying contemplated. A city is perhaps one of the most complete materialisations of the life of men and history. Few manifestations so completely include time and present, the throb of life.

> *The public space has this ambivalence, this capacity for permitting the experience of the intimate and sharing life with others.*

Although it's a slippery concept, could you tell us what exactly defines the city and how it differs from public space?

The whole city is public space *par excellence*. What distinguishes city from home would be what establishes the difference between public and private. The city accommodates the private but it's really the set of all the spaces of citizens, and this is the beautiful thing about those cities in which the private has no place. There shouldn't be any restrictions applied to life in the city. I don't think doors should be put on cities. Railway stations are the epitome of public space as they have never had to close their doors. In this regard, public space covers everything from a street to a park. When architects present their projects of parks and gardens for this Prize and do so in such a wholesale way, aren't they issuing a warning of what we are talking about now? Which are the buildings of public vocation? The private is linked with the sensation of property you have when you open the door of your home, but there are also cultures where the doors of houses are left open. I'd like to associate the private only with intimate life. Public is where you're totally available for others, while in the intimate realm you're only concerned about yourself. The dichotomy between city and home is what makes citizens of people. The house remains as the last redoubt of the intimate. The city is everything that does not affect the life of the intimate: all of that is city; all of that is public space.

One might think of public space as those places in which people cohabit. Public space doesn't have to be associated with places that have a certain crowd capacity. Large public gathering spaces have less sense today, or they only have it as spectacles in themselves. The space of St. Peter's in Rome is at once a place in which the notions of crowds and hierarchy come together. Sometimes there is confusion when the public domain is understood as territory where the masses can be comfortable, but the masses can be comfortable in very different ways: you can feel very content on a Sunday morning in the El Retiro park when it's crowded but this doesn't mean that El Retiro isn't fantastic, too, when you're there alone. The public space has this ambivalence, this capacity for permitting the experience of the intimate and sharing life with others.

Your long experience of teaching at Harvard University must have given you an exceptional standpoint from which to view what is happening in the architectural domain in Europe. How is the European city perceived from the United States?

The American city is less organic, more abstract than the European one. The European city can still be explained with the metaphor of a city that has the attributes of a body. In Europe one can still make out what would be the belly of the city, and what would be the head and its members. With the American city, everything is more inorganic. The inorganic condition goes with newly constructed cities. We can simplify a lot by saying that the American city is the garden city plus downtown. This American city very well reflects how much the individual and respect for his or her rights inspire American society. In the European city, the individual is included within numerous social circles that, while they curb his or her freedom, offer security and support in precariousness. This occurs to a lesser extent in the American city, where the individual is more alone, something that doubtless reflects the dichotomy between the single-family-home city and the downtown zone understood only as the city of business. Yet generalisation always makes one uneasy. Cities are so different. New York is almost a European city. If books, music and art are loved in a city, then it is a city like New York. But let's go back to what I wanted to say. In general terms, it would be this solitude of the individual that would prevail in the American city, in a society that, on the other hand, tends to give so much value to its institutions. The great invention of America is institutions, whether they are universities or cultural and aid organisations connected with philanthropy and this is because, since social circles are weak, individuals trust in the elective affinities that are set up through institutions. In them the nerve centre of social life is to be found.

I've sometimes said that the European city comes from the encircled, walled city but not the American city because the walls are already there with the Atlantic and the Pacific. They are cities that haven't needed to protect themselves, haven't been required to give a sense of closing from their very layout. Without this awareness of limit, the American city can have less form and hence greater abstraction. The huge dimensions of America, moreover, explain why it is no accident that the Americans have found support in the telephone, the aeroplane and the mass media, making them consubstantial with their way of life. In the end, America has had to find the means whereby the whole country can live together. It may be that the new mass media make it possible to feed the fantasy that America, in its immensity, is one single city.

A Decade of Awards
DIETMAR STEINER

The past ten years of the biennial European Prize for Urban Public Space are not only a testament to advances in terms of honoring outstanding architectural achievements, but they have also accompanied the discursive development of the meaning of public space over the past decade. Since its beginnings in 2000, a continually increasing process of cooperation began with other European architectural institutions. The prize winners and the archive have thereby provided a view of the development of urban public space in Europe that is both unique and representative.

As a member of the jury since 2002, I will attempt to portray the development of the Prize and the activities of the CCCB as a distilled reflection of the European debate. First of all, there is no other European city that can compare with Barcelona as a location for discourse on public space. The now legendary program for public spaces implemented during the 1980s was, after the political blockade of the Franco dictatorship, an act of urban liberation causing a worldwide sensation beyond the world of architecture.

So what could be more obvious than for the CCCB, a unique institution devoted to comprehensive cultural and intellectual development, to conceive and award a prize for urban public space? The numerous and varied project entries have constantly confronted the juries with several substantive questions: What is urban public space in the new millennium? Has it not long since vanished in the medial space of Internet communities? Hasn't urban space become increasingly privatized in reality? And hasn't it become ever more domesticated and disciplined by a growing number of rules and regulations?

We often forget that it was not until the second half of the 20th century that urban public space was defined as a generalizing type. Prior to that, the terminology of city planning only contained the concepts of streets and plazas, parks and recreational areas. It merely concerned the empty spaces between buildings required for fire safety and light. And in those cases where public space was considered and planned in terms of architectural 'shaping,' then only for the representation of political might – be it royal, fascist or communist – and in order to allow the behavior of the users of that space to be controlled and monitored. Not until the democratic reforms in the middle of the 19th century did the notion of public space 'for all,' of 'everyday publics,' emerge. But even this concept was determined and shaped by sociologically defined rituals, that is, political rituals.

Dietmar Steiner, director of the Architekturzentrum Wien in Vienna.

Hence, I dare to argue that there has never been and there will never be a free urban space for all actions and representations of the public. After all, each and every public space – as is especially apparent in the 'social space' of the Internet – is determined by rituals of use, which necessarily entail codes of behavior, limits of access and processes of exclusion. Jury president Manuel de Solà-Morales once expressed this point clearly and matter-of-factly: every football stadium is private, and yet all of its users, even though they have to pay to enter, have the feeling that they are using public space.

In reality, therefore, it doesn't matter whether urban public space is under public or private management, nor whether it constitutes real or virtual space. Every point of access and activity in this space requires 'political negotiation.' Left-wing complaints about the growing privatization of public space – the transformation of plazas into shopping malls – cannot withstand reality. I sit in a restaurant in a Barcelona shopping mall, which opens out onto a public-private space. I order a beer and spend an hour reading a book, without being bothered. I walk along the public space of the Passeig de Gràcia, until public security forces suddenly barricade the sidewalk due to a minor demonstration. My conclusion: the public use of public space is not a question of abstract relations of ownership, but is always a question of how power is exercised over that space.

It is this question of how to define urban public space that the jury members have been faced with over the last decade. Does public space have to be an open, outdoor space, or can buildings also be public space? Even the legendary Nolli Map of Rome (1748) shows that public spaces stretch from streets and plazas to the internal spaces of public buildings. Is a covered market, a church, or a shopping mall public space? Rafael Moneo, a President of the jury that awarded the 2010 prize to the Norwegian National Opera & Ballet in Oslo, offered an especially piquant justification for the flexibility of the concept of public space: The public space offered by the roof and the surroundings of the building is such an enrichment for Oslo's public space that the role of the building itself in that context becomes irrelevant.

What value do we assign to architectural and artistic projects that thematize public space in an ephemeral or temporal fashion? Indeed, these projects have become ever more important in recent years. These mostly participatory artistic projects convey increasing uncertainty about generally accepted rituals for the use of public space in increasingly heterogeneous societies. This artistic avant-garde hints to us that in the future, it will only be possible to 'moderate,' rather than determine, the use of public space. This means that the rituals of power and the rituals for appropriating space will come to flow together into a continual political discourse.

The public use of public space is not a question of abstract relations of ownership, but is always a question of how power is exercised over that space.

If I were to summarize my experience as a member of the jury, then I would have to address the technical process of evaluating entries. The jury always had to make decisions about the nature of the various entries, which have always been composed of images and texts. There is a real question as to whether brief recorded glances can truly give a sense of the long-term functionality of an urban public space. After all, these spaces take on life through the use that is made of them, and that use in turn depends on the seasons, on societal developments and political restrictions. All of this can only be verified through long-term observation and analysis.

On the other hand, the remarkable continuity within the jury has allowed an accumulation of knowledge about the significance and quality of entries. Currently popular elements of public space are floor lamps and dramatic lighting concepts; informal water surfaces, often with interactive foundations that playfully spray playing children; benches and seating areas; and ornamental floor spaces decorated with various patterns and materials. What is decisive is not how 'beautiful' a new public space has become, but whether it can tell a 'story' that can contribute to the identity of the location.

And sometimes, faced with 'before & after' images, it would have been better not to do anything at all. Urban public space is 'social sculpture,' a political space for negotiation. That is the 'text' that accompanies the discourse of the jury beyond the presented 'images.'

The *Flâneur's* Surprise
Lessons from the European Prize for Urban Public Space 2000–2010
DAVID BRAVO

An abandoned parliament building, a rubbish dump, a watchtower, a library, a pavilion-cum-theatre, a vegetable garden, the space under a motorway slab, an opera house, a cluster of lifts, some fishermen's huts … Doubtless, these are not exactly the kinds of scenes the 19th century *flâneur* we all bear within would have expected to find among the prize-winning works and special mentions over the six awards of the European Prize for Urban Public Space. The square, the street, the promenade and the park are the classical, almost canonical types that seem to be closest to the idea of urban public space. They bring together conditions that, at first glance, seem necessary and sufficient to represent it. More than anything else they are urban voids, exceptional discontinuities of the constructed mass. When we imagine a city without squares or streets, and hence without facades or doors or windows, we grasp the topological indispensability of these interstices. They define the geometric limits of private property, order it, structure it and connect it with the flow of people, goods and information while letting it receive sun and ventilation and get rid of its rubbish. These vital functions ensure that archetypical public spaces are open, that they take shape at ground level, that they are universally accessible and that their ownership is unquestionably public.

However, when we begin to probe the concept of public space a little, we realise that it is impossible to pigeonhole it into specific formal types. What happens, for example, to the canonical square when there is a curfew? Its physical and geometrical properties are not in the least altered and yet no one would hesitate in denying it the condition of public space. Whatever its name may seem to indicate, public space is not a geometric, Cartesian and objective framework, nor even a physical, material and tangible container. It is a subjective place, loaded with political content, which implies urbanity or, in other words, it is defined by the fact of coexistence in community and hence by awareness of ourselves and respect for others. It is, like democracy, something fragile and intangible that comes about intermittently. And, just as a parliament isn't democracy, the square isn't public space: in fact, both reside in the civic consciousness of citizens.

David Bravo, Barcelona-based architect and secretary of the 2010 European Prize for Urban Public Space.

This contingency, this autonomy with regard to form, explain the continuous production in our cities of a splitting between the *urbs* – the hardware, the containing physical support – and the *civitas* – the software or the contained event-. Public space is a dynamic, unstable occurrence that spreads out and contracts, that waxes and wanes in intensity. Because of this intermittency, it is necessary to keep striving continually to reconquer already built-up spaces that have lost their urbanity. Among the outstanding projects presented for the Prize there are interventions in squares, parks and esplanades, settings that comply with the classical patterns of public space. Yet they are not there because of the typology of their settings, formerly banal and featureless, stripped of the sense of urbanity and deactivated as public spaces. They are there because of the value and meanings they have regained.

Without moving from the site, a square in the Barking neighbourhood in London acquired the centrality of a main square by means of the eccentricity contributed by a series of eclectic, picturesque elements that cater to the collective imaginary. Without any change in its proportion, the Heroes of the Ghetto Square in Krakow ceased to be a space that was offensively indifferent to its dreadful past to become a place of recognition poetically narrating collective memory. In both the double square of Robbiano and the main square of Kalmar, which conform to the traditional model of squares presided over by churches, the intervention stays close to a classical theme, the ground level itself, not to decorate it with capricious formality but rather to ensure that it expresses, in the former case, the collective uses that the place might accommodate and, in the latter, the language of the cobblestones that have shaped the body and image of the whole city over centuries. In both Kalmar and the Smithfield Public Space of Dublin, also coming under the heading of classical squares, the reconquest has been preceded by ousting the private vehicle, a clearing up operation that has not altered the basic layout but has rather revealed them as clear spaces full of possibilities for the holding of community events.

Neither is it surprising to find among the notable works of the Prize open spaces that fit urban archetypes that are almost as classical as the square. The seafront esplanade in Zadar and that of Benidorm have undergone vigorous transformation working in favour of a sense of urbanity. The former resolves the meeting of city and water with a set of steps that invites crowds to enjoy contemplating the sea and listen to the music performed by the water itself. The latter unfolds in a pattern of colourful, sinuous forms with sufficient power to temper the speculative effervescence of the skyscrapers competing for the seafront, civilising them in a unitary embrace. In Rotterdam, few pedestrians ventured on to the central pavement of Westblaak Avenue until it was turned into a skateboard rink and an appealing meeting place for skateboarders and spectators alike. Without being subjected to any morphological transformation, the streets of Folkestone have been filled with personal experiences through a public exhibition of photographs contributed by its inhabitants.

If all these interventions have introduced a sense of urbanity into pre-existing archetypes, others have started out from much more accidental situations. The geographic barrier represented by a ravine or a difference in level can lead to the construction of a bridge or stairway that, over and above its connecting function, can take on monumental significance. This is the case of the lifts in Teruel that complement both the function and the monumentality of the stairway of the Paseo del Óvalo. There are also accidents of less natural origins, defects or impurities that the *urbs* itself generates in the course of its permanent metamorphosis. Sometimes they are vacant sites that are waiting to be filled with new civic uses. The Lene Voigt Park in Leipzig is the result of the citizens' conquest of the former site of a railway station destroyed in the Second World War. The Tilla Durieux street-salon in Berlin celebrates the emptiness of the strip created by the obligatory separation imposed by the Wall, while offering yearned-for space in the recently built-up surrounding area, a recreational area, like a green beach. A crevice between two buildings, which was not apt for construction, was taken over by residents in a Paris neighbourhood who planted a collectively run vegetable garden. The demolition of the Can Mulà textile factory opened up a wide, open space in the old centre of the town of Mollet, offering the unwonted opportunity for rethinking the centre of an already-consolidated town.

On other occasions, however, accidents in the urban fabric are not open empty spaces that can more or less easily be converted into archetypical public spaces but alien bodies, troublesome presences that also offer the opportunity of being assimilated for *civitas*. In this case, we are confronted with built-up volumes, which might be disconcerting when it comes to considering them as public space. Yet, when they are covered and have facades, they do not cease to be fully loaded with a sense of urbanity if it is understood that this sense is autonomous from the form. In Zaanstadt the motorway slab that split the centre of Koog aan de Zaan was turned into a great civic arcade that was able to accommodate the requirements of the citizens' different programmes. In Berlin, the Volkspalast initiative neutralised the symbolic charge of the abandoned GDR parliament building by temporarily converting it into an experimental cultural centre.

Pre-existence is not a necessary condition for a built-up mass to contain public space. If we accept the autonomy of the concept *vis-à-vis* forms and types, a newly-

All these interventions demonstrate that the concept of urban public space transcends the type, the scale and the situation of the container wherein it is found.

constructed building, too, can be impregnated with a feeling of urbanity. The construction of a row of fishermen's huts has equipped a breakwater in the port for a very deep-rooted local activity in Cangas do Morrazo. The Homage Tower in Huéscar restores the dual function, as both landmark and lookout, of an old watchtower. The former orients the residents within the urban fabric of the town, constituting an icon that commemorates a shared historic past, while the latter offers a point for enjoying a panoptical view from which the town is recognised and becomes aware of itself. Through very different means but with similar effects, the different sections of the roof of the Oslo Opera House gently emerge from the waters of the port to offer pedestrians, who can walk freely all over it, an iconic meeting place and attractive lookout over the city and fjord.

The Norwegian opera house demonstrates that, with the help of certain public functions, the iconic charge of a single, isolated and compact architectural object can exercise a dynamising influence over its wider urban context. In Copenhagen, the insertion of a forcefully present floating platform now enables citizens to enjoy healthy, accessible and safe bathing without leaving a canal which is full of significance for their city. Somewhere between clear space and building, the open-air library of Magdeburg made the most of prefabricated pieces from the façade of a demolished building, thereby achieving a powerful iconic charge and rising as an emblem of a promising future for the run-down neighbourhood of Salbke. In Innsbruck, a single building containing a series of community facilities has managed to forge deep centrality in an insipid residential estate that was notable for its lack of public space despite the abundance of public land. In Rotterdam, the insertion of a small theatre-pavilion in front of St. Lawrence Church has programmatically activated a lacklustre square.

If the concept of public space is defined by a sense of urbanity that makes it independent of forms and types, it is also free of restriction of size or scale. The results of the Prize reflect the capacity of some interventions to go beyond the scale of a square, an esplanade, a park or a building to take in a whole area of the urban fabric. In Espinho, a holistic intervention founded in the aims of improving urban space, providing better public facilities, rehabilitating the town's historic legacy and recovering natural resources has had transcendental effects in its improvement of the physical and social reality of an isolated, decaying neighbourhood. Along similar lines and with a strategy that is in keeping with the urban scale, a series of concise surgical operations have reinforced the physical and social cohesion of Buenavista del Norte.

Besides injecting urbanity into an existent *urbs*, operations on the urban scale can also civilise spaces that are not built up. Flooding of the Gállego River in Zuera, the River Ter in Girona, and the River Besòs in Barcelona created zones not apt for construction that the urban fabric had been incapable of assimilating. The conversion of these three river beds into fluvial parks maintains and reinforces their character as natural spaces, external to the *urbs*. Yet, at the same time, it fully integrates them into the *civitas* of the adjacent cities in offering their inhabitants a close-to-hand chance for escaping the urban hustle and bustle. Somewhat similar but in a much more extreme position, is the case of the Begues rubbish dump. Its remote natural setting makes it difficult to understand why it might be deemed urban space. However, apart from its conversion into a public park that generates energy and fulfils a significant educational function, the *raison d'être* of this piece of infrastructure is inseparable from the metropolitan reality that brought it into being and that it served for over 30 years.

All these interventions demonstrate that the concept of urban public space transcends the type, the scale and the situation of the container wherein it is found. If its condition of space and its condition of being urban are not always evident, neither is its public status. The action of the state, of the public sphere, excels in its capacity for injecting urbanity into high-cost productions of sweeping scope, for example those of Mollet, Espinho, Oslo or Benidorm. On other occasions, nonetheless, civil society is obliged to emancipate itself from the upside-down protection of the state when confronted with its negligence. This is particularly reflected in cases like the Volkspalast in Berlin, the Magdeburg Library or the vegetable gardens of Leipzig and Paris. Their existence does not culminate with the physical construction of a designed object, but is continually developed in an ongoing social, cultural and political production. Here, the citizens take the initiative for the project's development, participate in its conception, work together in the construction and even control its use and take over its management. In these situations a sense of urbanity, along with a capacity for coexistence, is especially reflected and this is what the notion of public space implies. And, to the surprise of the *flâneur*, this sense constitutes its single necessary and sufficient condition.

2000—2010

TEN YEARS OF THE EUROPEAN PRIZE FOR URBAN PUBLIC SPACE

PROJECTS

Map of the European Prize for Urban Public Space (2000–2010)

ELÍAS TORRES

Elías Torres, architect.

2010

Magdeburg

Open-Air Library

KARO* WITH ARCHITEKTUR + NETZWERK

—[JOINT WINNER]—
2010

Books against Depression
PETER CACHOLA SCHMAL

When this small project was awarded joint winner with the Oslo Opera House by the jury of the European Prize for Urban Public Space, presided over by Rafael Moneo, I was not that surprised, as this delightful project has been stirring up quite a bit of press dust in Germany in the past years, while evolving from a grassroots installation into a real building. Members of the jury commented that this project just did everything right you can do right in architecture at the moment. This was viewed already as being a little suspicious. Are not so many politically correct ingredients a sign of a calculated strategy? But what are these ingredients? A small piece with an open social nature was built in the difficult district of Magdeburg-Salbke, a typically derelict and shrinking city in former socialist Eastern Germany, marked by a vacancy ratio near 80% and a high unemployment rate of around 20%. This project was planned with the participation and even enthusiastic support of the local community, including some youth groups. It recycles architectural façade elements. And it places books in its centre of attention, for 24-hours free use in the main public square of the district. And this impressive spatial object is not only a great success with the public but it also looks really good, it is elegantly designed and balanced, it is fresh and appealing to architects – countering the notion that grassroots projects generally have a dreary pedagogical image.

Yes, the Leipzig-based collaborative KARO founded by the architect and freelance collaborator at the Bauhaus Dessau Foundation, Stefan Rettich, the architect Antje Heuer, and the mechanical engineer Bert Hafermalz did everything right, but they also risked a lot. The genesis of the project that their authors describe as 'situative urbanism' shows a slow evolution rather than a strategic marketing concept at work. Like so many other derelict public spaces in Eastern Germany this one, too, is in danger of being taken over by bored and notorious right-wing youth gangs. But this project was not generated by a top-down approach that could later easily fall prey to negligence and vandalism – just the opposite. It was the result of a patient social intervention process that started back in 2005. For a few days the central square – where in the 1980s the local library had actually been standing before it burned down – was inhabited by a spatial sculpture built out of 1,000 beer crates, following workshops of developing possible design approaches for this site together with the local community. Calls for book donations brought in around 10,000 books for this event that ended in poetry slam sessions and readings by authors. In the following years these book donations doubled in size and were used in an informal citizens' library set within a neighbouring unused store. The potential of the project managed to attract public funding within the federal government's program of 'experimental urban planning schemes', and the permanent building could finally be realized in June 2009.

The Open-Air Library, locally known as the 'Salbke Bookmark', comes very close to the very first beer-crate simulation, with its interior situated on the former central square well sheltered from the street. The beer crates have been substituted by aluminium façade panels that are not only iconic, as they stem from the shopping center façade system of the 1960s Horten chain – but they can also be read as a re-use of a typical Western consumerism symbol for Eastern social action. A small covered stage also serves a public function. Both the patio and the stage have been widely accepted and put to use by the citizens who have organized themselves to take care of their open library. The youth groups use the open space as their public meeting ground, since there is nowhere else for them to go in town. When the first attack of vandalism occurred recently, the people were aware of its meaning and defended their space. They organized the repairs and thus propagated a strong signal, that they would not tolerate such actions.

Stefan Rettich, the most public figure of Karo, stated that a lot of the recently emerging 'public spaces' in Eastern Germany are mainly leftover residual spaces in the urban fabric produced by the demolition of disused buildings without any favourable impact, pointing to the problem of the sustainable maintenance of these important spaces. With the Open-Air Library, Karo found a very original answer to this topic that is both convincing and invigorating. Therefore this project rightly deserves the 2010 European Prize for Urban Public Space, as it is exemplary for all other European cities faced with the problem of shrinking.

Peter Cachola Schmal, director of Deutsches Architekturmuseum (DAM) in Frankfurt.

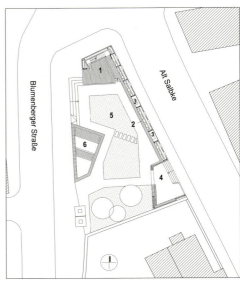

General plan. 1. Stage / 2. Bookwall / 3. Seating unit / 4. Youth-corner / 5. Lawn / 6. Terrace

Like so many other urban zones of East Germany, the district of Salbke in the southeast of Magdeburg is sunk in deep physical and social dereliction. The unemployment rate is high and its post-industrial landscape is scattered with abandoned factories, empty lots and a large number of vacant business premises and homes. In this setting, the site of the district's former library saw, in 2005, the beginnings of an urban planning experiment called 'City on Trial', promoted by the residents themselves.

The abandoned premises of an adjoining shop were used as a working space for organising the book collection and to draw up, in an open and neighbourly participative process, the programme for designing a new open-air library and listing its needs. Some 20,000 books were collected and, with over a thousand beer crates, a 1:1 scale model of the resulting proposal was constructed on the site. This then became the venue for a small poetry slam and readings festival. The success of the initiative helped to procure from the Federal Government the necessary funds to construct the facility, which was opened in 2009. Prefabricated pieces from the façade of a recently demolished 1960s building now shape a thick wall that holds the bookshelves. The wall, topped by a higher section that houses a cafeteria, shelters a green space where people can read in the open air and there is also a stage on which primary school plays are performed, public readings are given and concerts by young people's bands are held.

Open 24 hours a day, the facility is managed by the residents who, without any kind of monitoring or checks, freely take and return books. Although there has been the odd episode of vandalism testifying to the tough surroundings, the new library is fully-functioning. The residents have taken over a rundown space to turn it into an innovative meeting place that, with its powerful iconic charge, rises as an emblem of a more promising future for Salbke.

PROJECT **Open-Air Library, Magdeburg, Germany**
DATE **2009**
AUTHORS **KARO* with Architektur+Netzwerk**
SURFACE **488 m²**
COST **325,000 €**

North elevation

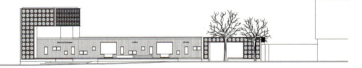

West elevation

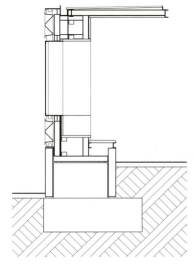

Section detail

Oslo
Norwegian National Opera & Ballet
SNØHETTA
[JOINT WINNER]
2010

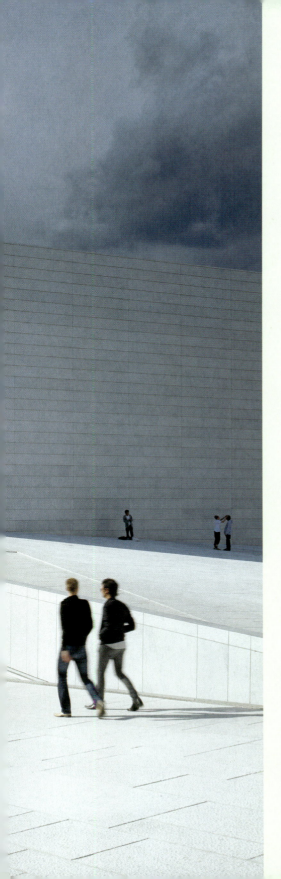

The Unobtrusively Monumental

KJARTAN FLØGSTAD

From nature's point of view the Norwegian capital lies at the very end of a fjord. Bjørvika is the innermost bay at the head of the Oslo fjord. This is as far as the sea can reach. It is in this deep indentation of the ocean that we find the new Norwegian Opera House.

Many of Snøhetta's building projects can be found in such locations, in the transition between land and sea, between the ocean and solid ground. Here there were once quays, wharves, boat traffic, moorings for ships, the loading and unloading of cargo and passengers. Architects intervene by building new cultural arenas and thereby changing these historic meeting places. The opera house in Bjørvika too is located in a traditional harbour area, which is today in the process of being gentrified and renamed Fjordbyen (Fjord town). As in harbour towns all over the world, the scrap heap of industrialism is being transformed into a palace of consumption. Our senses ring in time to the cash registers. Industrial culture becomes the culture industry. The wheel of fortune replaces the sprocket wheel as the driving economic force.

In itself an opera building in an old harbour area is a spectacular expression of gentrification and the late-modern transition from industrial culture to culture industry. According to the ideology behind the transformation of the old harbour towns, the closed docks are being reopened for the town's citizens. This is also what Fjordbyen claims. But at the same time as it opens inwardly, Fjordbyen closes itself off from the world outside. The docks stand idle, the ocean-going vessels loading and unloading elsewhere than in the town centre. As shipping winds down, so does direct contact with the world beyond. By catering to the needs of the cultural bourgeoisie, Fjordbyen becomes the harbour town that turns its back on the world and turns in on itself.

The saloon itself is fashioned along classical lines, modelled on La Scala, almost the Stradivarius of the opera house. But the great feat of the Oslo Opera is that it is not only, and perhaps not even primarily, a concert hall and a politico-cultural emblem. Right from the beginning its external forms have been put to use and taken to heart by the whole town, regardless of opera interests, as a public arena. By opening for egalitarian, democratic and non-commercial use, its external form becomes its most important content. The opera house lies there on the seafront, like a glacier calving or an iceberg hitting land, drawing the line of vision landwards towards the characteristic hills behind the city centre. Also in this respect the building is a reminder of the architects' verbal signature: Snøhetta means Snow Cap.

The Twin Towers of Manhattan's World Trade Centre were potent architectural expressions of late-modern utopianism. The skyscraper of steel, glass and concrete was both capitalism's and socialism's attempt to build their way to heaven. Although Snøhetta's landmark buildings point in a different direction, they are not primarily anti-utopian. At the same time they are fundamentally different from the World Trade Centre and Burj Khalifa in Dubai, which with its 800 metres is now meant to be the highest building in the world. When Snøhetta lays its monumental buildings along the ground, like flat, horizontal skyscrapers, it is not laying to rest the notion of soaring aspirations, but rather giving our late-modern dwellings a new earthly foundation.

With its precipitous and extremely undulating terrain, Norway appears as a sort of natural skyscraper landscape. Highly conscious of this topographic point of departure, Snøhetta take the vertical and the towering as a given and create buildings that carve earthbound forms, cutting across both the natural conditions and technological utopianism.

In this way Snøhetta's monumentality often becomes an unobtrusive monumentality. The Library of Alexandria in Egypt, another of their landmark buildings, creates a negative space in relation to the buildings around it. You don't see it until you're up close. The same will probably be the case with the opera house in Bjørvika when the docklands around are fully developed, with office buildings following a strictly commercial rationality. In many ways Snøhetta's opera house can be seen as a draft of a different sort of modernity to the one that proved so vulnerable on Lower Manhattan that fateful day in September 2001. The opera house in Bjørvika makes its mark at both a natural and an ideological point of intersection. The architecture has grasped the external, the superficial and the spectacular aspects of operatic art, and created an arena in which to act out physical and social roles in the open air, on the roof of the opera building.

Kjartan Fløgstad, Oslo-based writer; his recent novel is Grand Manila *published by Éditions Stock, Paris 2009.*

Built around a cove of the Oslo fjord, the port neighbourhood of Bjørvika is the historic centre of the capital. Despite its central location, by the end of the 20th century, the large buildings constructed to give infrastructural support to the port's commercial activity had ended up segregating it from the rest of the urban fabric so that it would become a marginal area. The Norwegian Government decided to turn the zone into a representative neighbourhood that would attract a lot of visitors and articulate the relationship between city and fjord. The first step in this transformation was to be achieved with the construction of an opera house on a wharf adjoining a busy highway and the railway lines that run together as they enter the nearby central station.

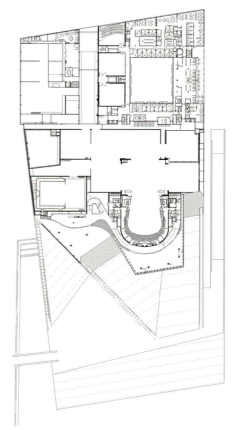

Third-floor plan

Accessible only by means of a walkway that crosses the adjacent highway, the roofing of the new Opera House forms a series of gently sloping planes that, rising from the waters of the port, ascend over the concert hall. The slopes, covered in white Carrara marble, are totally open for people to walk on. Their disposition generates several spaces suitable for strolling around, for holding open air shows and contemplating the splendid views over the city and fjord.
Independently of the activity that might be taking place inside the building, the roof, with its different parts, has become an appealing and popular meeting place. The gentle encounter of the sloping planes with the water gives visitors the sensation of being on a beach, while the height they can attain as a result of the ascending surface offers them a splendid lookout over the city and its scenery. The slope that makes such attributes possible does not, however, involve any indiscriminate appearance of protective barriers but rather it opens out in a perfectly natural fashion, respecting the freedom and intelligence of the people walking there. With the majestic presence of an iceberg, the new Opera House rises as a symbol of a new Bjørvika which presides with dignity over the meeting of city and fjord.

PROJECT **Norwegian National Opera & Ballet, Oslo, Norway**
DATE **2008**
AUTHORS **Snøhetta**
DEVELOPER **Statsbygg, The Ministry of Church and Cultural Affairs**
SURFACE **38,500 m²**
COST **500,000,000 €**

Longitudinal section

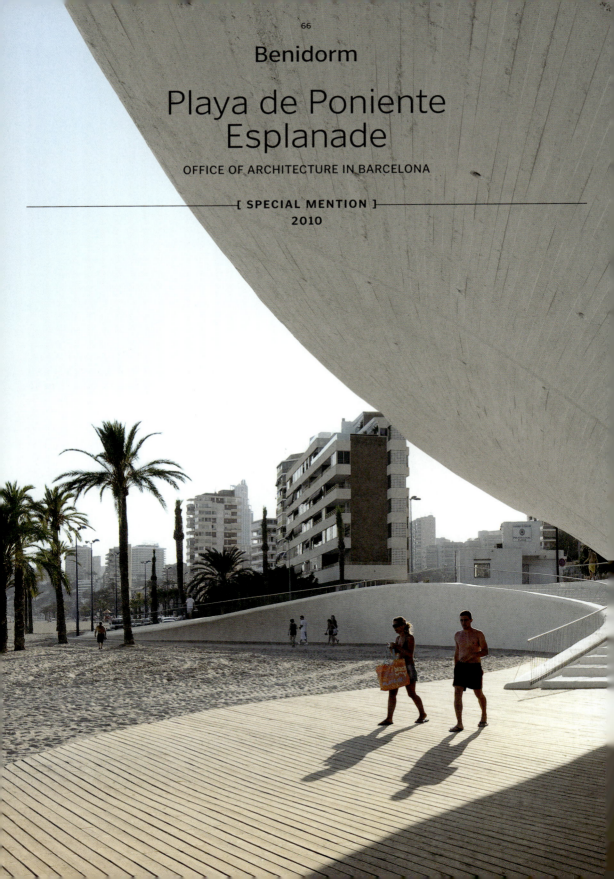

Benidorm

Playa de Poniente Esplanade

OFFICE OF ARCHITECTURE IN BARCELONA

— [SPECIAL MENTION] —
2010

Waves in Colours
JOSÉ MIGUEL IRIBAS

One of the factors that distinguishes the Spanish tourist offering is that, apart from a few lamentable recent exceptions, it has been established on the basis of urban structures since – unlike what happens with the resort model, which is extrinsically mimetic and intrinsically monotonous – cities always achieve a high degree of singularity and this is a key component for finding a differentiated niche, and hence one that is intelligible to consumers in the international market.

The city is, then, the most powerful and fertile setting for consolidating a tourist destination in the long term, as well as limiting its vulnerability to novelty and short-lived fads.

In those tourist zones where, like Benidorm, the urban personality is so well defined (since, however controversial it might be, it achieves very firm attachments and is thereby guaranteed a high degree of stability), the permanent reconstruction of collective space is a decisive factor in maintaining the thrust of the tourist industry, despite the fact that there have been no outstanding operations in this domain in the last 25 years because the public sector has clearly lagged behind the private sector in the process of regenerating the overall tourist offer.

In urban-based mass tourism, collective space is a key element in shaping the product so that the cities of best scenic quality tend to be those most highly rated by tourists (under the pressing condition that they are also fun). Their better quality has immediate economic effects in generating greater demand. Hence, in being part of the productive system, the urban setting should be perceived as a remote and indirect but also a secure and profitable factor of production in such a way that its constant regeneration becomes an objectively indispensable requirement.

Besides constituting an imperative that is conceptually assimilable to any city, positive intervention in collective space has, in the case of Benidorm, an added component that should not be underestimated. For many years now the street has clearly come before the beach in the consumption and space/time preferences of tourists, and people spend more than four hours a day in the former. Hence collective space, in this city, is the most fundamental component of the offering.

Finally, the existent imbalance between the two Benidorm beaches, both with regard to how often they are frequented and the degree and quality of their urban development, made it obligatory that the project should resolve the difference by constructing a space that would not only meet demands and rectify the problems and conflicts over the beach and its immediate urban environs – which was already pledged – but that it should also undertake, albeit partially, the goal of restoring the balance between the city's two beaches in their symbolic importance and ability to attract people.

The project of the Playa Poniente seafront esplanade in Benidorm is highly positive in its strategic urban planning content, for the specific setting and for the city as a whole, no matter how much consideration of these strategic factors is only implicit. Although it is a space contending with the beach and the sea, which do not appear as clearly as they should as the main contents of this space, the esplanade more than adequately resolves the functional conflicts while also substantially improving the immediate urban space and managing to convey an idea of Benidorm that is very pleasing to its public since it identifies in good measure with the cultural and generational content that the city had in the crucial phase of its urban development. It is a sixties-style project, cheerful and colourful, as befits a city that, with its recovery of the popular festival (lost or shunted aside in European industrial spaces), has created the conceptual core of its tourist offering.

It is not surprising, then, that it should have been indisputably successful as far as the clientele is concerned. Maybe this is not sufficient for escaping nit-picking of the academic navel-gazing variety where any social success is suspicious in itself. This is a deplorable attitude since it is evident that any collective space must comply with the necessary morphological and functional demands and it is also obvious that it attains full legitimacy when it is able to attract the public and when its frequenting is achieved in the most efficient, low-cost, open and dynamic way.

José Miguel Iribas, Valencia-based sociologist, specialising in tourism analysis.

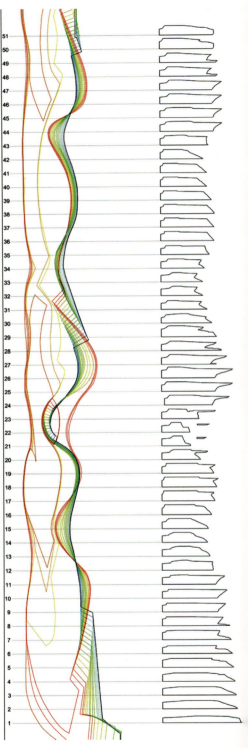

Final layout

The esplanade of the western beach of Benidorm once ran for one and a half kilometres parallel to a four-lane road and a long line of above-ground parking spaces. In the 1970s it was covered with mediocre paving and lined with a heavy concrete balustrade, 1.2 metres in height, which considerably obstructed the view of the sea. Access to the sand was only possible by way of ostentatious imperial stairways set 200 metres apart. The new esplanade has reduced the urbanised surface, creating a complex strip of transition between city and sea. It is structured over a sinuous succession of white concrete walls delimiting terraces, flowerbeds and ramps with a line of apparently capricious concave and convex geometric surfaces that, in fact, are subject to a strict modular system. Garden plots and the interplay of different colours in the paving fill in the sections separating the walls in their undulating coming and going. The road has been restricted now to two lanes and an underground parking area runs longitudinally along the esplanade. The architectural barriers have been eliminated, markedly improving access to the beach by way of a good number of stairways and ramps.

Once again, Benidorm is posited as an urban paradigm within the industry of mass tourism. Its extreme density is concentrated in an area of land that is significantly small in comparison with the large extensions of territory taken up by other more disperse models of sporadic occupation and almost unviable maintenance. It is precisely this density that makes possible the concentrated investment of large amounts of public money in projects such as this. The esplanade's colourful surging forms evoke the gardens of Antoni Gaudí or Burle Marx, while its powerful iconic presence unfolds in a forceful embrace with the skyscrapers along the seafront, ordering them into a unitary body.

PROJECT **Playa de Poniente Esplanade**
DATE **2009**
AUTHORS **Carlos Ferrater Lambarri & Xavier Martí Galí (Office of Architecture in Barcelona OAB)**
DEVELOPER **Generalitat de la Comunitat Valenciana and Benidorm City Council**
SURFACE **40,000 m²**
COST **10,620,000 €**

Cangas de Morrazo

Fishermen's Huts

IRISARRI & PIÑERA

—[SPECIAL MENTION]—
2010

Horizontal Choreography
SARAH ICHIOKA

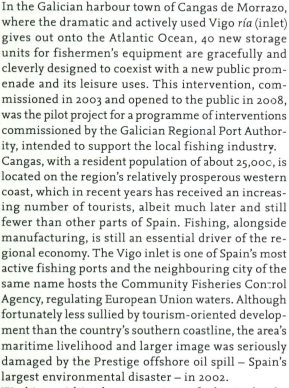

In the Galician harbour town of Cangas de Morrazo, where the dramatic and actively used Vigo *ría* (inlet) gives out onto the Atlantic Ocean, 40 new storage units for fishermen's equipment are gracefully and cleverly designed to coexist with a new public promenade and its leisure uses. This intervention, commissioned in 2003 and opened to the public in 2008, was the pilot project for a programme of interventions commissioned by the Galician Regional Port Authority, intended to support the local fishing industry.

Cangas, with a resident population of about 25,000, is located on the region's relatively prosperous western coast, which in recent years has received an increasing number of tourists, albeit much later and still fewer than other parts of Spain. Fishing, alongside manufacturing, is still an essential driver of the regional economy. The Vigo inlet is one of Spain's most active fishing ports and the neighbouring city of the same name hosts the Community Fisheries Control Agency, regulating European Union waters. Although fortunately less sullied by tourism-oriented development than the country's southern coastline, the area's maritime livelihood and larger image was seriously damaged by the Prestige offshore oil spill – Spain's largest environmental disaster – in 2002.

Working within the constraints of a limited public budget, regionally based architects Jesús Irisarri Castro and Guadalupe Piñera Manso have artfully combined the fishermen's functional brief for net and tackle storage with Cangas residents' expressed desires for new, flexible public space. The resulting intervention on the Calle de Dioco de Arrigo, a rock-piled breakwater extending west-east in parallel to Cangas's historic seafront promenade, artfully choreographs the coexistence of multiple uses that would otherwise have potential for friction, including impromptu 'marine events', a car park, a yacht club, a boat-launch ramp, pier, and pedestrian access to the beach.

The intervention's visual dominance, stretching 215 metres along the length of the pier, makes a confident

assertion of its importance as a new element within the built environment. However, while the structure maintains a strong, unified presence when viewed at oblique angles, its metal mesh cladding fulfils its architects' intentions that it 'dissolve' into the landscape when viewed at a cross or frontal perspective, avoiding too aggressive a blockade of the view into or out from the town centre to its north.

The south-facing facade is porticoed, bordering a continuous new public boardwalk offering views out to the mouth of the *ría*. A half-storey lower, the northern elevation, facing back towards the city centre, gives the fishermen access to boats moored below.

The 40 fishermen's storage units come in three different sizes. These are arranged in 11 groupings of three to four units with each cluster sharing stairways, patios and courtyards for services and outdoor work, encouraging collective activities amongst their users.

The narrow, water-bound breakwater offered limited room for construction, necessitating prefabrication of components, which were then assembled on site. The structure is made from galvanised steel sheeting – particularly durable in the harsh marine climate – and polycarbonate panels. A metal mesh at varied densities unifies the structure, shaping intermediate zones between the storage units, communal working areas and the fully public spaces, and allowing a level of transparency. According to Irisarri & Piñera, the material was also chosen to harmonise with the port's changing blue and grey skies. The concrete underfoot contains seashells from the local canning industry.

Strategically built around a bay of the Ria de Vigo, the port of Cangas is home to intense nautical and fishing activity that is not in contradiction with the beauty of its environs. It is closed on the southern side by a breakwater consisting of two rectilinear arms meeting at an angle to form a walkway more than 500 metres long and offering good views of the town from the sea. On the inner wharf of the breakwater, there is a yacht club, a road for vehicular traffic, an above-ground car park and moorings, while the side facing the river is lined by an esplanade and a dike made of large blocks of stone, which is frequented by rod-and-line fishermen. The entity that manages the ports of Galicia promoted an intervention with a view to constructing a row of 40 fishermen's huts on the breakwater along with a new public walkway. Made of galvanised steel plates, the huts allow the fishermen to store their tackle and avail themselves of the outside working spaces. The line of huts is interrupted by ten transversal passageways that connect with the inner wharf where the boats are moored and with the outer dike used for rod fishing.

General plan

The walkway that runs along the dike, thus enabling passers-by to watch the fishermen's activities, has been paved with a platform of wooden slats.
Despite the specificity of its beneficiaries, the project brings life to the breakwater as a public space, organising the setting around an activity that appeals to everyone, besides being one that is deeply rooted in the everyday reality of Cangas. The tasks and tackle pertaining to this popular activity invade the neutral and contained minimalist structure of the huts conferring on them an air of vitality that changes with time.

PROJECT **Fishermen's Huts, Cangas de Morrazo, Spain**
DATE **2008**
AUTHORS **Jesús Irisarri and Guadalupe Piñera**
DEVELOPER **Puertos de Galicia**
SURFACE **3,920 m²**
COST **1,200,000 €**

As with most newly completed architectural interventions there is a certain apparently wilful cleanliness about the project's presentation in published photographs. If this is to be an active place of work for individuals, some capacity for personalisation (and with it, disorder) is necessary. However, this is a minor quibble and no doubt fleeting condition, as the robust plainness of the galvanised steel structure both promises durability and suggests the generous potential for adaptability and customisation over time.

The structure's unapologetic modernity and durability avoids any romanticisation of the fishing trade as a nostalgic relic or as a secondary attractor for the tourist industry.

Nevertheless, the project appears to succeed in accommodating and reconciling the needs of at least three distinct groups: workers (fishermen), locals taking recreation, and – presumably – elevated numbers of visitors attracted by the performative visibility of the intervention. The confident interweaving of functions surely benefits from locally embedded knowledge; Irisarri & Piñera have practiced from their studio in the neighbouring city of Vigo for the past 20 years.

By demonstrating how an urban public space that proudly features places for locally embedded economic activity can generate delightful spaces for leisure and contemplation, and integrate their respective users, the project's client and architects offer a positive alternative example of coastal development, particularly poignant in a Spanish context.

Sarah Ichioka, director of The Architecture Foundation, London.

Rotterdam

Urban Activators
Theatre Podium & Grotekerkplein

ATELIER KEMPE THILL

[SPECIAL MENTION]
2010

The City's Stage

HUIB HAYE VAN DER WERF

St Lawrence Church is the only medieval building in Rotterdam and therefore the oldest standing structure in the entire city. Having been started in the mid-15th century and not attained its current robust stature until the mid-17th century, the church itself is a symbol to the perseverance of its patrons and the role it plays in the social and cultural fabric of the city of Rotterdam. It has seen buildings come and go, rivers and canals dammed and rerouted, destructive force indiscriminately being dropped from the sky, as well as countless city-councilors disputing over the past and future shape of the city. Throughout, the church and its stature have remained a solid and constant factor in the city's identity and skyline.

When contemplating so much history and transformation, however, it is strange to consider the peculiar structure that now stands on the Grotekerkplein immediately before its doors. At the west-end of the square – in between the main entrance of the church and the Delftsevaart waterway – stands a roofed elongated pavilion open on its two main sides with two square compartments on each end, raised just slightly higher than the surrounding square. This object at first seems to have fallen from the sky. The structure's minimal form offers a clinical contrast to the late-gothic style of the church itself, but also to the typical end-modernism of the adjacent buildings. Its light-grey concrete quality also has little relationship with the predominantly brick characteristics of the surrounding square. All the while the form itself – a strong horizontal structure with a roof stretching over a span of 50 metres – seems placed on the surface of the square but not fully rooted in the surroundings. The steps to ascend the pavilion's stage seem to accent the notion that to do so means to board an object just slightly hovering over the ground.

But then – as with many things, on second glance – a relationship and purpose begin to reveal. It becomes evident that the architects – Atelier Kempe Thill – have been quite precise in their design and positioning of the pavilion in terms of the balance it has with its surrounding environment. Its elongated quality emphasizes the waterway running just next to it, as well as the Blaak market plaza on the other side of the church. This horizontal character provides a strong contrast to the verticality of the church tower (which is only 14 metres higher than the pavilion is long), thereby creating a perpendicular stability between the two objects. Finally the synchronicity between the design of the Grotekerkplein itself and the positioning of the pavilion is subtle yet impressive. The open space of the square – still intimately framed by the surrounding buildings – reveals the clear balance between the pavilion as a stage and the square as the space for a potential audience.

It is then that one realizes that this is not simply a piece of street furniture that latently offers itself to the citizens of Rotterdam as a place to sit or skate on, it is a podium in every active connotation of the word, which is exactly what the commissioning body – the Rotary Club of Rotterdam – had in mind when holding a competition for the square. They sought to invigorate with cultural activity what had become a rather desolate public square, for on each side of the square behind its surrounding buildings run busy shopping/market streets that had left the Grotekerkplein isolated without a function or reason to stay. Thanks to Atelier Kempe Thill's bold yet open (almost transparent) manifestation, the square has gained a certain intimacy and presence. When programmed, the architecture acts as a podium that draws visitors and facilitates cultural action. When not in use, the structure acts as a pavilion for leisure and urban recreation. More so, because of its open quality it acts as a frame for its surroundings. Because it has no rear it does not turn its back on the city. Rather, it outlines what is behind and in front of it thereby emphasizing its environment. If there is one thing to be said about the structure as a negative result it is that what it frames is not always a pretty picture. It becomes painfully clear that the buildings across the waterway have turned their backs on the square and church, and that buildings on the square itself do not share the same open quality of the pavilion/podium. However, even there lies the positive and activating potential of this architecture. Thanks to this framing, more citizens will see that much can still be done to change their surroundings. They may realize that an initiative such as that atoned in realizing the Urban Activator Theater Podium can lead to cultural activation but also structural change. Both lead to a better city. Already the church is being renovated and stands as a strong comrade together with the podium. When finished both should be witness to the coming history of an active, urban Rotterdam.

Huib Haye van der Werf, curator Nederlands Architectuurinstituut (NAi), Rotterdam.

Bombing attacks in the Second World War levelled almost all the buildings surrounding the Grotekerkplein, the old main square of Rotterdam. Despite its privileged position between Sint Laurenskerk (St Lawrence Church) and the Delftsevaart canal, the mediocrity of the adjacent buildings constructed after the war gave it the feel of a backyard. A theatre pavilion has now been constructed with a view to programmatically activating this dull, unappealing space. The building has a prismatic volume and runs parallel to the canal to close off the western end of the square. It consists of two cubic nuclei resting on a podium and sustaining a 50-centimetre-high, 30-metres-long slab. The result is a great horizontal gateway framing a stage that is open on both sides. A 70-metre-long running curtain hanging from the edge of the roof makes it possible to have performances facing the square or the canal, and the curtains can be closed on both sides at the same time to create a closed hall. The lateral core buildings offer storage

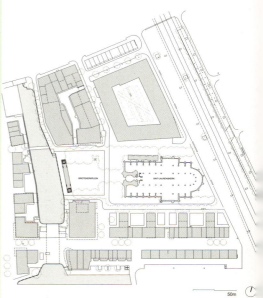

Location

space, toilet facilities and a dressing room for the artists. Besides equipping the square with a new focus for public events, the pavilion rises as a structure with the twofold value of acting both as an opaque limit reinforcing the perimeter of the Grotekerkplein and as a threshold significantly connecting it with the Delftsevaart.

PROJECT **Urban Activators Theatre Podium & Grotekerkplein, Rotterdam, The Netherlands**
DATE **2009**
AUTHORS **Atelier Kempe Thill**
DEVELOPER **Rotary Club Rotterdam Noord, Foundation 'Grotekerkplein', OBR Rotterdam**
SURFACE **10,000 m²**
COST **1,150,500 €**

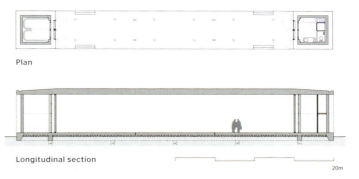

Plan

Longitudinal section

20m

Passage 56, Espace Culturel Écologique

Paris

ATELIER D'ARCHITECTURE AUTOGÉRÉE

[SPECIAL MENTION]
2010

From the Interstice to the Interface

FRANCIS RAMBERT

Paris has a history with its passageways. They have inspired literature and nurtured thought about the city. But what would Walter Benjamin say today about the discovery of Passage 56 in north-east Paris? Because this is where we are, here, in the Rue Saint Blaise in the 20th arrondissement, far from the centre of the capital, almost on the boundaries of the Haussmannesque city. The ring road is just a stone's throw away.

This intervention on the suburban fabric of the city is part of a process geared to reconquering areas of urban neglect that is taking place throughout Europe, but which is a pilot scheme in Paris. How can we extricate ourselves from an impasse smoothly, how can we reactivate a site that cannot be used to build public space: this is the strategy used in this, the tightest of spaces.

This project by the Atelier d'Architecture Autogérée (AAA) sings the praises of microurbanism in a neighbourhood that «isn't easy». The challenge laid in the transformation of a small plot of land covering an area of 200m². The scale was one of proximity. The intervention was exceptional in more than one way. First of all, it sought to recreate the conditions of urbanity in a completely barren place. The passage in question was, in fact, used as a dustbin by the local residents who had adopted the unfortunate habit of throwing their rubbish into this fenced-off urban wasteland. Next, the work on this passage focused on the thread of a 'low-tech' culture: it was designed to be easy, or even obvious, to carry out.

Finally, it put into practice the principle of enclosure that didn't separate but sought, on the contrary, to connect. A visual link from one end of the plot to another, a social link between the inhabitants in a wider circle. The key word is resocialisation. This is how 30 families and a dozen associations have come to share this new space. Social practice is the key to this project whose spatial practice is based solely on uses. Several parallel activities can take place here, from gardening to political debates. There is no room for design in its layout. This is not the purpose.

The tightness of the plot, a space that is 6.50 metres wide and developed to a depth of 30 metres, between two gable walls, is expanded by its setting. The minimum seeks to be the creator of the maximum. A lightweight architecture of polycarbonate marks out the threshold of the passage which reveals a series of planted beds with the traditional 'garden shed'. Even if we are invited to grow here (organic vegetables of course), this type of intervention is totally different from the workers' gardens that are widespread throughout the Parisian region.

The architects – Constantin Petcou, Doina Petrescu, and their team – set out to design a device that would make it possible to produce (by solar roof panels) more energy than the users consume. Rainwater is collected and the rubble has been transformed into a garden by the landscape architect Agnés Sourisseau. The idea that brings everyone together is the development of the environmental potential of the place.

Things aren't frozen in this process, architects have even called for a 'blurred' concept. «To move from the urban *terrain vague* to *terrain* of urban *vagueness*, of urban indeterminacy,» as Constantin Petcou, who was one of the founders of AAA in 2001, puts it. This «more community-based than environmental» collective has actually been pursuing this goal for a decade in a spirit of «extradisciplinarity»: another word for cross-cuttingness. They thus look for a way to embark on a new practice of the city, often by starting from nothing but always with the involvement of the residents. It is within this «participative» framework that their ECObox came to fruition in Paris in 2004 from the perspective of creating a «network of eco-urbanity».

With the transformation of Passage 56, the AAA architects have shown that an unlikely situation can eventually generate public space, thereby opening up prospects and bringing a certain optimism. The lease signed with the social housing foreman (who has become a partner in the project) will run for five years. We have already arranged a meeting to evaluate this intervention that was conceived as an invitation to appropriation.

Francis Rambert, director of La Cité de l'Architecture et du Patrimoine, Paris.

Rue Saint Blaise runs through the 20th arrondissement of Paris, a neighbourhood notable for its urban density and cultural diversity. The deterioration undergone by this pedestrian precinct in recent years has brought about a decline in its public uses, the closing down of businesses, social segregation and insecurity for children and the elderly. At number 56 in this street there is a passageway that was closed off in the 1980s when a residential block was constructed and the space, which was not amenable to further construction, remained shut off and neglected ever since.
In an unusual association between the public administration, local organisations, professionals and residents, an open process of consultation was organised in order to discuss in a public forum suggestions, possibilities and misgivings related to the site. This gave rise to the idea of a collectively managed space that could be the venue for meetings, film screenings, workshops, games, intercultural exchanges and activities revolving around gastronomy and horticulture. By means of a continuous participative process, a project was drawn up and constructed with minimal cost and using recycled materials collected by the residents themselves. The result is a wooden construction with a garden cover and a green office hanging between the two buildings that flank the space, thus constituting a lintel between the public space and the new garden with its plots for collective cultivation. The project as a whole has solar panels, compost pits and a rainwater collection and storage system so that it is almost self-sufficient in the water, compost, food and energy it consumes.
The Passage 56 project reinforces the idea that public space does not culminate in the idea of the physical construction of a designed object but is continuously developed as a social, cultural and political production. Here, the client does not precede the intervention but gradually emerges in the group of people who manage it, offering irrefutable proof that everyday ecological practice can transform present spatial and social relations in a dense and culturally diverse metropolis.

PROJECT **Passage 56, Espace Culturel Ecologique, Paris, France**
DATE **2009**
AUTHORS **Atelier d'Architecture Autogérée (AAA): C. Petcou, D. Petrescu, N. Marchand, F. Ralaimongo, G. Barraud, S. Pauquet, R. Binder**
DEVELOPER **Atelier d'Architecture Autogérée with DPVI, Mairie de 20ème, Paris Habitat and group of neighbours from the Saint-Blaise area**
SURFACE **200 m²**
COST **90,000 €**

Diagram showing uses by years

2008

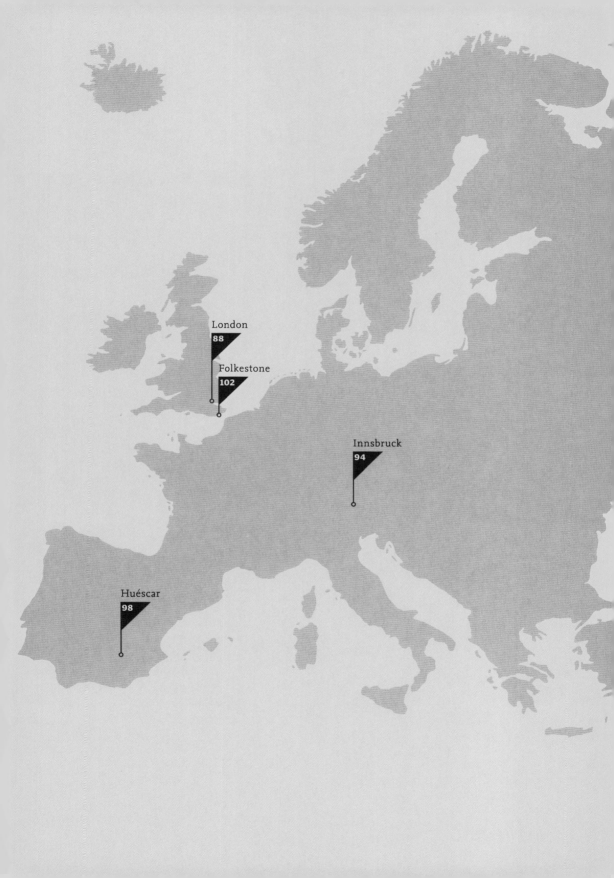

Return to the Picturesque
BEATRICE GALILEE

On the very outskirts of London, 15 miles northeast from the city centre, Barking is a town once famous for its flourishing port and fishing industries. In the 19th century this gave way to heavy industry and manufacturing. At the turn of the 21st century the town was synonymous with a bleak post-industrial landscape of unemployment, deprivation and political extremism.

It was in this context that Barking was pinpointed as part of a major regeneration scheme for affordable homes and new commercial centres along the Thames Gateway. The town centre was also selected as a site for the Mayor of London's flagship '100 Public Spaces' project, which aimed to rejuvenate town centres across the capital.

The selection of muf to produce a town square masterplan was enlightened. The London-based office started in 1996 with an interdisciplinary agenda to fuse art in the public realm with an architectural approach that investigates social and political issues, prioritising process and research over design and building. They have produced a discourse of ideas and language about place shaping and identity that is peerless in the UK.

The square allocated to muf is a rectangle flanked on three sides by brand-new, brightly coloured apartment buildings designed by London-based AHMM and on a fourth by an old brick library. When approaching the site, the studio had to answer several questions: how to create a feeling of 'the local' in a new town centre? How to create a relationship to history and context in a brand new space with a confused and disparate past? To produce a design that encourages a synergic relationship with surroundings, the diverse communities of local people and encourage them to stay there, to feel comfortable without resorting to a tiresome didactic of a palate of tasteful materials, forms and colours.

Instead of a single concept, muf have chosen to answer these questions with a number of distinct elements each with their own individual qualities and which are linked by a mass of pink granite across the square.

The first is a dazzling black and white arcade on the ground floor of one of the new apartment blocks. Giant diamonds of monochrome terrazzo zig-zag along the ground like a super-sized version of an Edwardian London doorstep. Above them 13 bright golden chandeliers designed by Tom Dixon hang from the double-height ceiling adding unexpected grandeur and style.

The arcade spills out onto the salmon-coloured paving of the square. Large circles containing young and old trees are cookie-cut from the ground and occasionally filled with jazzed up terrazzo as a few of Dixon's golden chandeliers are strung between the branches and hover between the trees. A rich green arboretum meanders through the middle, creating a varied and dense atmosphere that usefully conceals the brightly coloured balconies of the immediate surroundings. In amongst the wooden decks and ivy-covered walls, muf commissioned bespoke benches designed by students from the Royal College of Art, a large timber stage, new bins, drinking fountains and installed public WiFi.

At the corner of the square, 'The Secret Garden', the most curious of their interventions, stands. Named after the children's novel in which an overgrown wall is discovered to conceal a world of unimagined beauty, muf's 'Secret Garden' is a 7-metre-high wall made from a variety of dusty-red and yellow reclaimed bricks. Built by local college students, it is littered with strange artifacts from architectural salvage yards: gargoyles, a coat of arms, a ram, an impassable doorway. Muf describe it as a 'folly', which it is. But unlike the intentions of the newly built ruined castles which were positioned across the English countryside by Victorians to prettify landscapes, this prominent presence, forming a backdrop to their square, seems wonderfully strange and unexplained.

What is interesting about muf's response in Barking is that the seemingly incongruous nature of their interventions – an arcade, a folly and an arboretum – together create an atmosphere that is warm and quite unexpected. With the use of subtle symbols of comfort, shelter, calm, grandeur and history, these scattered mementos ensure none of the intimidating newness that can render such developments unused and unloved. Instead they trigger an instantly habitable picturesque space of human scale, of undoubted eccentricity and definite success.

Beatrice Galilee, London- and Berlin-based independent writer and curator.

After years of neglect, Barking's urban fabric has been transformed by major construction work, while recent tensions between newcomers and the existing population have affected its social fabric. Barking needed a new civic space that would rescue a lost identity from the past and project into the future a space where the community could come together. The area of level ground in front of the Town Hall, which was previously used as a parking space, has now been transformed into a centrally located, well-equipped main square that is full of shared meanings. Besides the Town Hall, the new square is flanked by a library and a Learning Centre, while the fourth façade is a 'Folly Wall' which hides a supermarket boundary and, in resembling a ruin, evokes the exposed brick facades of Barking's old buildings. The square is connected with the borough's main shopping area by way of an arcade illuminated by chandeliers and tiled with black and white paving slabs that hark back to London's magnificent Georgian houses. Alongside the arcade and the square is an arboretum with 40 mature trees of 16 different species that are lit up at night with colours that vary according to the time of year. The eclectic combination of all these picturesque and extravagant elements counters the banality of an urban landscape that had lost its attributes, giving the space the colour of new meanings and making of it a recognisable and meaningful place. Surprisingly, it is eccentricity that has brought centrality to Barking's new main square.

PROJECT **Barking Town Square, London, United Kingdom**
DATE **2008–2010**
AUTHORS **muf architecture/art, Allford Hall Monaghan & Morris**
PARTICIPANTS **Atelier One, Atelier Ten, Buro Happold, Beattie Watkinson, Spread the Word**
DEVELOPER **Redrow Regeneration on behalf of London Borough of Barking and Dagenham**
SURFACE **6,468 m²**
COST **2,620,000 €**

General plan

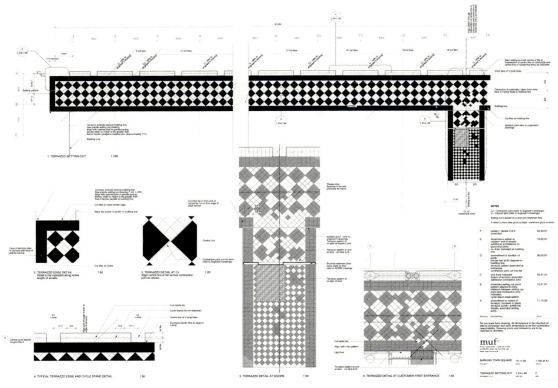

Detail of paving

Prunus serrua Tibetan cherry	*Prunus autumnalis* Winter flowering cherry	*Prunus avium plena* Wild cherry	*Betula jaquemonti* Himalayan birch	*Betula nigra* River Birch	*Alnus Glutinosa* Alder	
Juglans Regia Walnut Tree	*Robinia Pseudoacacia* False Acacia	*Salix tristis* Willow	*Populus Tremula* Quaking aspen	*Quercus palustris* Pin oak	*Taxodium ascendens nuttans* Swamp cypress	

Catalogue of trees

A considered decision was made to match the bulk of the building that surrounds the public space with mature trees up to 12 metres tall on planting. Also mature trees tend to be found in the privileged west of London.

They are arranged in informal clusters grouped as ceremonial backdrop woodland with its attendant fragile ecology and the melodrama of swamp cypress and hillocks.

Innsbruck
Centrum.Odorf

FROETSCHER LICHTENWAGNER & IDEALICE

[SPECIAL MENTION]
2008

Internal Growth

GABRIELE KAISER

The Olympic Village at the Eastern edge of Innsbruck, erected in two stages for the Winter Olympics in 1964 and 1976 as a monofunctional recreational development for about 8,000 inhabitants, has struggled with many problems typical of peripheral residential areas: lack of infrastructure, a shortage of cultural offerings and adequate spaces for social interaction, aging, etc. If the Olympic Village with its high-rise towers was controversial among experts even at the time of its construction, its status has hardly improved over the years. The occupants of this quarter, crammed in between two major roads on the north bank of the Inn, complain especially about rising traffic noise caused by the random construction of shopping malls on the borders of the city. Furthermore, the homogeneity of the inhabitants, the lacking generational and social diversity, has contributed to the desolation of the quarter. The worn-down community center hardly seemed attractive, and the scattered remaining spaces between the residential buildings failed in spite of their generous scale to convey any sense of generosity or cohesion. The 1996 international competition Europan 4, under the heading 'Town upon the Town', granted Innsbruck a welcome opportunity to engage in the construction of a new city center in the Olympic Village.

The leitmotiv of the competition – Internal growth, instead of consumption of land – between up-and-coming architects provided an ideal set of circumstances for reinvigorating an urban quarter. The winner was a project proposed by Froetscher Lichtenwagner (its first work under this name), whose proposal confronted the existing context directly by engaging in its morphology at different levels and in a discrete mimetic fashion. The project, which the Europan Jury termed an «unsentimental statement», pays respect to the existing modernist structures, whose meandering formation exercises an angular hold on the space it creates.

The architects realized immediately that it would be impossible to meet the challenge of forming a city center within an already existent city context, 'Town upon the Town' – by architectural means alone. From the very beginning they envisioned the project as an integrative task that could not be managed without a sensitivity for the overarching structural context. Though the original Europan draft featured greater density and a more intensive functional mixture than the final revised project, even the ultimate implementation demonstrated the intense efforts of all involved to rejuvenate the quarter in a socially sustainable fashion. Public space in the low-rise, diverse living forms in the tower. The public spectrum in the low-rise (a branch of a Tyrolean supermarket chain with a café, event hall, kindergarten and youth club) creates a certain basic frequency in the plaza, which together with Alice Grössinger, a landscape architect, was designed partly as an urban street space and partly as an ironic variation on an Alpine garden theme. The diagonal white stripes that radiate out from the passage between the low-rise and the tower, as well as the wave-form benches, break up the geometry of the rectangular plaza, which can also be seen as an extension or revision of the existing green spaces. A shadowy pent roof and arches provide for additional spatial differentiation in the expansive plaza. One can cross the plaza, but it's even better to use it as a true outdoor recreational space (provided the weather cooperates). A life that once «seemed to get lost in the interstices of housing complexes and officially landscaped spaces» can now easily unfold in the new center of the Olympic Village.

Gabriele Kaiser, architecture journalist and curator at the Architekturzentrum Wien, Vienna.

Many of the housing estates that were built in the peripheral areas of European cities in the 1960s and 1970s are characterised by an abundance of public land and scarcity of public space. Such is the case of the neighbourhood constituted by Innsbruck's two Olympic villages, which were constructed side by side for the Winter Olympics of 1964 and 1976. These new extensions were rapidly planned and occupied in such a way that both the urban landscape and the settlements themselves present an almost isotropic uniformity in which it is not easy to identify significant places of collective meaning. This intervention has established a new, well-equipped, recognisable and accessible urban centre between the two villages, joining their physical and functional areas and bringing them together in a new meeting point. The focus is a multifunctional building that concentrates public facilities, housing and offices around a new square. Totally and exceptionally derived from its centralising function, the new construction is not at odds with the neighbourhood landscape, even though it is readily identifiable within the typology of the surrounding buildings.

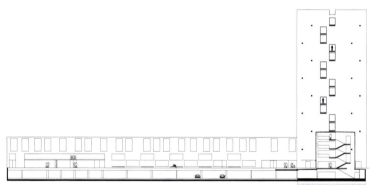

Longitudinal section

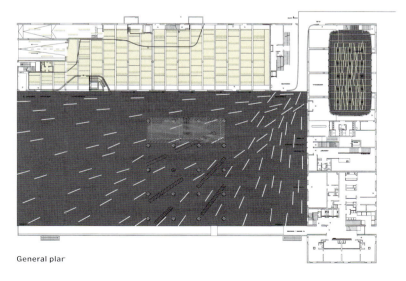

General plan

PROJECT **Centrum.Odorf, Innsbruck, Austria**
DATE **2006**
AUTHORS **Froetscher Lichtenwagner in collaboration with IDEALICE (Alice Grössinger)**
PARTICIPANTS **Willi Froetscher, Christian Lichtenwagner, Leszek Liszka, Petra Gorjanz, Christian Lindner**
DEVELOPER **IIG Innsbrucker Immobilien GmbH & Co KG**
SURFACE **24,200 m²**
COST **23,000,000 €**

The Actuality of the Past

LUIS GARCÍA MONTERO

The present is a meditation on the past. This does not mean that we are condemned to live in observance of the rules of bygone days, in compliance with the shadows that the bulk of time loads on our backs. What happens is more like the opposite. The past depends on us, needs us, forms part of the imagination of the present. The gaze of today sees the streets, the corners, the fields. The ear of today listens to the music, the noises and the wind of reality. The skin of today feels the play of lights and darknesses. The gaze, the ear and the skin of today think the past, a past that forms part of the present, a past that is actuality, the actuality of the past.

In its deep sense, then, any kind of restoration turns out to be impossible. Social and political systems that attempt to restore a custom, an ideology, a system, abandon themselves to the lie, creating a hypocritical distance between the official representation and the real existence, forcing a kind of *costumbrismo* of nostalgia that not only paralyses the present but falsifies the past. The only way of becoming sensitised to history is to read its traces and interpret them from the present. Rendering homage is a commitment to reality, not a restoration of what has disappeared.

I have known Antonio Jiménez Torrecillas' work since his Nasrid Wall intervention in the Alto Albaicín zone of Granada. Now I see his impressive project of the Homage Tower in Huéscar become reality. Looking at the solutions achieved by this admirable architect, I reaffirm the idea that the past is no more than a proposal that the gaze of today makes reality. We need to make the past ours, interpret it, give it meaning, turn it into an exercise of imagination and concept.

The Tower speaks to us of military surveillance during an epoch of frontiers in the Kingdom of Granada. The soldiers scan the horizon, seeking any enemy movement, dust rising from the fields, bodies flitting among trees. We can imagine the routine of the guards, their passing along the walkways behind the battlements, the rolling of the hours over spears and stones. We can imagine the urgency of the defence manoeuvres before an attacking army, a rushing of ramps, a bellowing of barricades. Eyes give voice to the alarm, setting off the preparations for combat.

Antonio Jiménez Torrecillas chooses this gaze to leave it alone, to clear it of mishaps, of conjunctures, of battles. A tower, whether in times of love or war, whether it is a familiar image or a tourist stop, is, more than anything else, an invitation to the gaze. One sees things from on high, confirms distances as eyes roam from distant mountains and green fields to village houses. The definition of the I is always a dialogue of distances and proximities. We need to lay the foundations of surroundings in order to construct a self.

With this intervention, this Granada architect has made his commitment to the gaze. He plays with ramps, uses palisades to reconstruct the feel of parapeted walkways so as to enable the circular sweep of steps and eyes. He purges the vestiges of the martial past and of reality just as poets purge the words of the tribe. It is all about feeling that one is accompanied by the present, or by the vocabulary, so as to be left alone with one's own gaze. There is the village, and there are the fields, the mountains and the sounds. There are the distances and the proximities. There is the natural and urban staging of uncertainty and quietude. But everything becomes surroundings as one becomes aware of the sense of one's gaze, in watching out not for the enemy but for one's own self.

Antonio Jiménez Torrecillas therefore invites us to move up inside the Homage Tower. The poet Juan Ramón Jiménez said that the human being – helped by architecture –, tends to grow upwards and outwards, and rarely grows inwards. This intervention transforms the tower into a defence of the gaze and helps us to move upwards, inwardly, to become the possessors of our own eyes. The play of light and shadow in the inner spaces, the bare walls, the view of the sky become blue clarity and intuition of loftiness, the ramps leading upwards embody the effort and the process of gaining authority over our gaze.

Art is a project because it is aesthetic emotion and it is concept. Learning to look, to defend one's own gaze, to become the owners of our consciousness; this is what the Homage Tower symbolises for me as metaphor. We know, we interpret, we become proprietors of the here and now, giving dignity to today and actuality to our past. The tower, before the immensity and the elements, is an image of each and every one of us.

Luis García Montero, Granada-based poet, writer and literary critic.

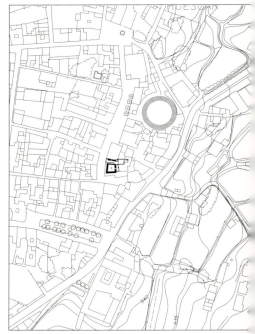

Site plan

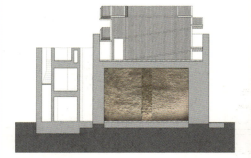

Section

Not far from the unstable frontier between Islamic and Christian realms, Huéscar changed hands seven times between the 13th and 15th centuries. This insecurity made it necessary to keep watch on the surrounding territory and the Homage Tower was the means for doing so until, in 1434, with the penultimate Christian conquest of the city, it was destroyed. Only its one-storey-high stone base remained so that, over the years, it lost its monumental character and was converted into a dwelling. Restoring the tower, then, could not mean physically restoring or shoring up an original form that had been lost in the oblivion of time. Thus, 600 years after its demolition, this project has, in a respectful and openly contemporary style, reinvented the form of the tower, restoring to it only the meaning and public function of a lookout. Before constructing it again, it was necessary to re-project it. This, then, is an abstract, non-figurative rehabilitation that has been able to make the most of the symbolic power of the old monument while freeing it of the tyranny of its pre-existing form.

PROJECT **Homage Tower, Huéscar, Spain**
DATE **2007**
AUTHOR **Antonio Jiménez Torrecillas**
PARTICIPANTS **M. J. Conde, M. A. Ramos, N. Torices, M. Guzmán, J. Valero - Jovagema, C. Tienza, M. Dumont, M. Panella, S. Pigeon, S. Betz, A. García, D. Arredondo, M. del C. Ramos, F. Fernández, M. Giraud, J. J. Sendra, J. M. López**
DEVELOPER **Junta de Andalucía, Delegación de Cultura**
SURFACE **810 m²**
DATE **550,230 €**

Folkestone
Other People's Photographs
STRANGE CARGO ARTS
[SPECIAL MENTION]
2008

Memory, Public Art and Urban Regeneration

XAVIER RIBAS

Family pictures are elusive statements, as family albums are complex documents. Paraphrasing Michel de Certeau, family pictures and family albums are 'full of shadows'. We look at them in ceremony, quasi-deferentially, searching, perhaps, for whatever signs of love may still be visible in them. We could say that family pictures and family albums are constructed out of love. This is partly what compels us to look at the back of these photographs: a search for the handwritten inscription of a name, a date, a place, or an intimate declaration of sorts. Words, then, are intrinsic to the family photograph, even if by absence, as absence itself is at the heart of family albums: their construction is also a process of demolition. This fascination for what is not there, for what has been lost or has been purposely cut out and erased, the manifestation of a desire to forget, is at the very core of any investigation into the family photograph, or into urban space.

In many ways, Other People's Photographs is an exceptional endeavour. It is a project that stems from the very heart of a place and its people. It is enthusiastic, celebratory, participatory… Most importantly, it got people and stories out of their homes, and into the streets. This migration of people and photographs from the domestic space into the street reactivates the social and political nature of public space. Private narratives become public statements, and the insularity of the home, and the shelved family album, is transcended. However, we could question what happens to the family picture when it is relocated as if it were a street sign, laminated against the weather, and mounted on metal plaques at vandal-safe height on a lamppost. How should we negotiate the legibility of this 'abstracted' image? Or, indeed, we could question whether there may not be a trace of violence in this displacement.

But Other People's Photographs is many things at once, or perhaps, consecutively. It starts with a black and white photograph of a young couple in a Folkestone street market in 1955, and it finishes not far away from the very place this photograph was taken, over 50 years later, at a 'memory bank' located in Albion Mews, an alleyway annexed to the new shopping centre of Bouverie Place. This phenomenal journey from the family album to the shopping mall is a significant one. Other People's Photographs is essentially a project about the city and about memory, of people as well as places. It was commissioned by the agents involved in the Bouverie regeneration project in the heart of Folkestone, namely Shepway District Council and the London-based corporate developers and owners of the new shopping centre: Bride Hall and Warner Estates. This collision of memory and urban regeneration adds a significant amount of possibility and complexity to the project that cannot be ignored, and somehow makes it, to my knowledge, unique.

Bouverie Place is described as a shopping centre, although in reality it appears to be only an elevated ASDA supermarket, with two levels of car park on top, and a number of chain shops at street level, the likes of Next, HMV, George, and Starbucks. These chain shops are aligned in what once was the continuation of Alexandra Gardens, which still runs through from Sandgate Road to Middleburg Square, except that now one end of the street has an ASDA flying over it. By the confluence of Alexandra Gardens and Albion Mews, the two touch screens of Other People's Photographs contain the project's bulk of pictures and stories. They look like a friendlier version of the Nationwide cash dispensers located a bit further along the same wall. As happens in private developments like Bouverie Place, the new shopping centre has replaced local businesses with chain shops at the expense of well-established local communities and local networks. In order to counteract this invasive presence, this 'void' of locality, and whatever history of displacement and confrontation with local dissidents may have occurred during regeneration, a certain historical 'depth' could be conveniently added to the place. In the new Bouverie, where erasure is complete, the ATMs of memory do the job, they bring back some historical resonance to the new site, transforming corporate ownership into carers for the local community, commissioners of public art.

The extraordinary energy and vision put into this project collapses in Bouverie Place, where the 'sanctuary of memory' fails to acknowledge a history of confrontation, displacement and erasure that went

As has happened with so many other cities, the urban landscape of Folkestone has undergone transformation over time with the appearance of new buildings replacing old ones while the underlying structure of the city's planning has remained unchanged. However, the ambitious Bouverie Place project has suddenly brought about a thoroughgoing, large-scale transformation. After years of demolition, construction work and land being used as parking sites, new buildings and public spaces have now been introduced into the city and these have to be recognised, assimilated and digested within the collective consciousness. With this in mind, the initiative Other People's Photographs has collected more than 540 photographs of people from among the community, taken over 125 years in the city's public spaces. The voice of the owner of each photograph has been recorded telling the story that goes with it. Every photograph has been repro-

Plan

duced on a metal support and hung in the space where it was taken. Children on bicycles, people proudly posing with a new car, street festivities... a whole series of personally-experienced everyday scenes are thus projected into the public sphere, thereby creating a huge photograph album full of memories and meanings that have now become collective. Two touch screens installed in Bouverie Place enable people to look at all the photographs, listen to the explanations and situate them on the map of the city. Today, the new square is the nerve centre of a network of memories extending all over the city.

PROJECT **Other People's Photographs, Folkestone, United Kingdom**
DATE **2008**
AUTHORS **Strange Cargo Arts**
DEVELOPER **Arts Council England, Bride Hall, Interreg III, Arts and Business, Shepway District Council**
SURFACE **4 x 7 km**
COST **315,000 €**

in the making of the shopping mall that now holds it. In the now privatised Albion Mews and Alexandra Gardens, where 'photography is not allowed without permission', the beautiful pictures and voices of Other People's Photographs become assets for the benefit of corporate business, hijacked and coffee-tabled, tamed to the point of conformity, to adorn the public image of ubiquitous developers and complacent local authorities. In its phenomenal beauty, Other People's Photographs represents a missed opportunity to become the most remarkable piece of local activism in the form of community public art. Bouverie Place, with its grey grandeur, its self-importance, and its ASDA warehouse of panoramic escalators and low wages, oblivious to the likes of Papas, Cowie and Turner, has managed to acquire public image at the expense of private photographs. And what is more, it has also acquired the copyright of the images.

Xavier Ribas, photographer and Senior Lecturer in Photography at the University of Brighton.

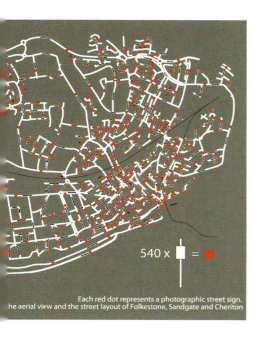

Each red dot represents a photographic street sign. The aerial view and the street layout of Folkestone, Sandgate and Cheriton

2006

Zadar

Sea Organ

NIKOLA BAŠIĆ

[JOINT WINNER]
2006

Live Infinity

ŽELJKA ČORAK

We are standing on the seaside of the town of Zadar. The sea moves like the arches on the fronts of Romanesque churches. The sun is setting towards what is said to be the most beautiful sundown in the world. Birds and ships make the picture complete. There are also young people in it, and many of them because Zadar is a university town. Until recently, they walked along the waterfront as the place to idle. Big cruisers come and cast anchor in the same picture. Curious people with good intentions will meet here the artistic heritage and the current life of this long-lived town. And as soon as they touch the ground, they will come face to face with a miracle.

Ahead of the town there is a magnificent archipelago, behind it a green fertile hinterland. The town dates back to prehistory, and in the Roman times it was a bustling Mediterranean harbour. Its urban structure is still determined by the Roman layout, upon which grew the picturesque mediaeval tissue. It is said that one only needs to put a hand in the sea to connect immediately with the whole world. But the sea was not always associated with only good things. When the crusaders in 1202 owed Venice transport costs, Venice obliged them to pay the costs back by conquering the Christian Zadar. They won this battle *en route* in the Holy War in spite of all the Pope's excommunications. Centuries of Turkish conquests also made the hinterland a dangerous area. Although facing infinity, many towns were however uncomfortable with it, and they lived an introverted life. But the unusual history of Zadar, which in many ways shows to Europe the other side of its face, continued in modern times. In the Second World War 80% of this town-monument was destroyed in the bombings of the Allies. In the recent war against Croatia, Zadar again went through difficult times. Modern architecture of the post-Second World War reconstruction adjusted extremely well to the urban matrix, but some gaps in vivacity still remained. A lot of archaeology came into the sunlight; the Roman Forum now spreads in the town centre, meeting the sea. However, this encounter did not release all of the energy of this place. And this energy should have been felt in order to move apart the boundaries of everyday life in the face of infinity.

Everything around us is a song, but we hear it rarely. Everything around us is interconnected into one holistic message, sound and light, a silent sliding of minutes. But we have forgotten that language – and also the velocity of transience, and the irretrievableness of a moment. Architect Nikola Bašić was standing on this shore as well, and heard a twofold sound: depth and distance. Aided by one of the most poetic intuitions in the contemporary formation of space, he translated the sound of the sea into music for the human ear. He shaped a part of the waterfront as steps descending gently into the sea, resembling a section of an ancient theatre and harmonious as the rhythm of organ pipes. Indeed, this is an instrument, and it was named Sea Organ by the architect. Underneath the sea surface there are hollows in the steps, and the movement of water masses through them is converted by sensors into audible sounds. Aleatoric God's score runs like the oscillogram of time, like the secret line of history in which there is no pause, in which the past flows directly into the future, and the possible place in the present time is only in our mind. Like Wagner's endless melody, like Ligeti's radicalization of Wagner, like the activation of silence, like the shading of volumes. Gentle blows of short tones, when a ship passes by, when an oar slithers, when a bird's wing grazes the surface. The composition has no end: it awaits us there always, and it guides us to listen closely to the world wherever we are – because by being an ear we become an instrument which hears itself. It seems as if Rilke had composed his poem 'Gong' on the Zadar coast, next to Bašić's Sea Organ.

However, the process of transformation of the wordless into the human did not remain in the area of sound only. By creating the complementary visual element to the Sea Organ, Bašić translated their sound with the help of sensors into light impulses. The result was the project Greeting to the Sun, the sun whose setting is at its most beautiful in Zadar. Every evening the sun performs its dance of light and shadows in the dark-blue glass circle, and the dance relates to a range of points in time – ancient Zadar saint's days from the mediaeval calendar, which are recorded at the brim of the circle. Sound, light, history and a moment in the life of a witness unite under the Sun, thus pointing to the relation between cause and effect.

Sometimes called the 'ship of stone' since it occupies an elongated peninsula, Zadar was heavily bombed in the Second World War. Post-war reconstruction failed to do justice to its 'prow' which, despite its wonderful sunsets, was not much visited. In 2004, with the incipient tourist industry in Croatia, the authorities decided to refurbish the zone as a wharf for incoming cruise vessels, whereupon the space went from neglect to having a key gateway role. Next, an esplanade was required to lead from the port to the city.

A stairway running along a 70-metre front bridges the difference in height between wharf and esplanade. This consists of seven juxtaposed flights of white marble steps gently running down into the sea, each section with a difference in height of one step vis-à-vis its neighbour so that the stairway as a whole offers a staggered silhouette reminiscent of the varying dimensions of the parts of a musical instrument. A series of tubes of different diameters and lengths run though the inside of each flight, connecting the submerged part with a gallery beneath the esplanade. With the thrust of the waves the water comes in through the lower end of the tubes, runs into the gallery and spills back into the sea. In this process, the air inside the conduits is propelled towards a series of orifices that emit a wide range of musical tones.

The Sea Organ dissolves the limits between sea and land, preserving a spacious transit zone between both spaces. The wharf is no longer an abrupt barrier protecting but distancing man from the sea. Rather, like a beach, it summons the coming and going of waves. The steps become a grandstand from which to contemplate the sunset while listening to music composed and sung by the sea itself.

PROJECT **Sea Organ, Zadar, Croatia**
DATE **2005**
AUTHORS **Nikola Bašić**
PARTICIPANTS **I. Stamac, V. Androcec, T. Heferer**
DEVELOPER **Zadar City Council**
SURFACE **1,700 m²**
COST **240,000 €**

The struggle with infinity is a motive of personal and transpersonal history, the existence of an individual and the existence of a town. *Horror infiniti* requires a great power of self-control. To face infinity means to face the real image of one's own soul. Architect Nikola Bašić created a contemporary space manifesting itself in the unity of physics and metaphysics, aesthetics and ethics. This should presumably be a good measure for the fullness of void.

Željka Čorak, poet and art historian.

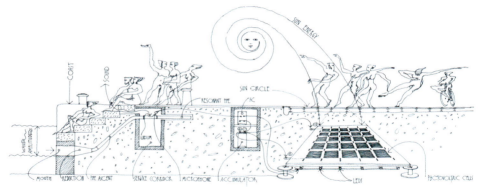

Sketch

Doing Most with Less
OLE BOUMAN

Few things are as driven by maximalism as architecture. The craft stands out for its almost boundless urge to prove itself. Success depends on the fullness of the portfolio, on the size of the projects, on prestigious clients, on a deluge of publicity, and, last but not least, on a certain type of personalities for whom enough is never enough. Unbridled ambition is the hallmark of the famous architecture firms and schools, where 'going home' is considered tantamount to giving up. For anyone hoping to escape the drudgery of just meeting the client's programmatic demands, sleeping under the desk is perfectly normal. If you want to become a thinking, creative architect, not only must you be capable of doing anything, you also have to do it. Work, work, work: that's the motto. But architecture is maximalist not only in this quantitative sense. It also has a penchant for maximalist designs – not lots, but huge. Many projects that were realized in the heyday of the architectural icon, seem confrontational rather than adaptive, filling airtime and screaming for attention. Often, it seems these projects revolve around filling a traumatic absence, both physically and morally. As if the void is an unbearable evil.

But a counter movement has emerged. The movement of doing less, sometimes even doing almost nothing. Projects have come into existence which aim at the exact opposite. They are small, subtle suggestions that do not aim so much to negate the emptiness as to mark it. This is not an architecture of the complete makeover and grand strategies, of retouching reality rather than adding a subtle touch. This is about an architecture that discovers that tactics are often the better option, that doing things is a question of degrees, of the right dose.

A8ernA, a project for a public space under the A8 driveway right through the city of Zaandam, is such an architecture. Exactly where high-speed logistics of car culture seem to have prevailed over the public qualities of pedestrian street life, NL Architects have discovered and invented space to live and breath again. In this obtrusive environment they have projected a set of public facilities that turn out to be

stronger and more attractive than the archetype of dehumanized wasteland: the neglected spaces under the notorious highway flyover. And so they made and environment for shopping, meeting, playing, relaxing, strolling and skating, on top of a continued deck that connects all facilities in one single gesture.

They acknowledged the brief in their own creative way, redefining the aims, suggesting the hidden potentials of the site. Much better than maximal design this project can be called generous design. It doesn't direct its use, it catalyses it. It encourages people to occupy and appropriate, a much more subjective version of using 'facilities'.

So modest is the intervention that the clients even seem to have forgotten that they needed architects to do it for them, that they couldn't do without architectural intelligence. On the official webpage that belongs to the area (http://www.zaanstad.nl/sv/a8ernahp/?view=Standard), they don't mention NL Architects at all.

Perhaps that's the strongest feature of this architecture of almost nothing. The design of public space becomes so transparent, natural and logical, that it seems to have emerged out of the ashes of derelict terrain as a gift of fate, not the product of hard work by a very intelligent office.

Intelligent they are. They saw opportunities in oblivion. They saw strength in decay. They saw joy in negative space. The most important quality of this design is to identify quality itself, where nobody expects it to be found. You need a supple mind, first of all; and then enthusiasm, bravura and determination to make it work.

Perhaps it is the European spirit that has inspired NL Architects. This mind shift becomes strongest, when it is directed to the transformation of public space. Against all odds, the European city keeps resurrecting as the urban DNA of the continent.

Cost of the miracle this time: 2.7 milion.

Ole Bouman, director of the Nederlands Architectuurinstituut (NAi), Rotterdam.

The A8 motorway, constructed in the 1970s, crosses the River Zaan to run, on 7-metre pillars, through the centre of Koog aan de Zaan in the municipality of Zaanstad. This impressive infrastructure passes over the main street, leaving the church on one side and the council chambers on the other. Beneath the slab a 400-metre-long strip was abandoned to messily parked cars for over 30 years.

In 2003 the council began work to restore the connection between the two sides. The document A8ernA was produced in a highly participative process so that it contained the requests of the citizens in a project that saw the presence of the A8 more as an opportunity than a problem. Its morphology and central riverside location meant that the slab could function as a large arcade able to accommodate the variety of wishes the citizens expressed. An open square occupies the centre of the strip. At the eastern end, a new quay with views over the river brings the water right up to the main street, speckling the underside of the slab

with its luminous reflections, while the western end has a children's playground, a 'graffiti gallery', a skateboard park, a break-dance stage, table football and ping-pong tables, futsal facilities, a basketball court and 'lovers' benches'.

Without changing its morphology, the motorway has become a great threshold joining the town in two ways, uniting its two halves with the river and gathering its citizens under a single ceiling that accommodates all the uses they have asked for. More than construction A8ernA is occupation, offering new content rather than a new container. As if furnishing an uninviting home, the pieces of the new project are fitted together in an eclectic, fragmentary amalgam that balances the unitary character of the porticoed slab.

PROJECT **A8ernA, Zaanstad, Netherlands**
DATE **2005**
AUTHORS **NL Architects, Pieter Bannenberg, Walter van Dijk, Kamiel Klaasse, Mark Linnemann**
DEVELOPER **Zaanstad Programme Management Dienst Stad**
SURFACE **24,000 m²**
COST **2,700,000 €**

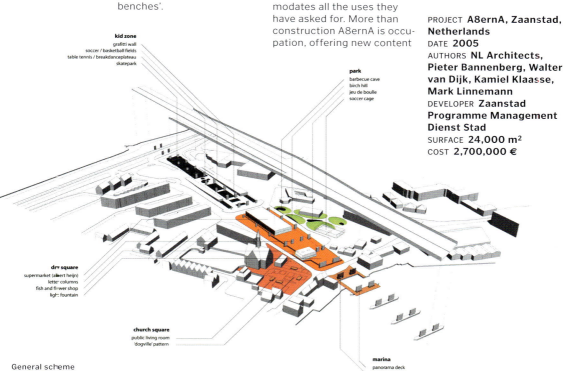

General scheme

Robbiano

Piazza Nera Piazza Bianca

IFDESIGN

[SPECIAL MENTION]
2006

Double Square

LUCA MOLINARI

Being called upon as urban planners to reflect on the nature of a contemporary town square is, I feel, one of the most challenging and risky issues for us to address today.

Over the centuries, Italian and European cities have inculcated in us a profound, almost 'natural', idea of what a square is supposed to be.

This is an image rooted for hundreds of years in the history of art, urban design and social mixing, which has transformed the idea of a square into an almost indisputable *topos*, arising out of a series of rules, proportions and habits that have been repeated and have undergone subtle variations for at least two millennia.

Yet the 20th century, despite all its stopping and starting, its breathtaking accelerations, its violent gear changes, was also able to question a whole series of key words that stand for places, spaces and consolidated habits, including, of course, the word 'square' [piazza].

The progressive loss of defined boundaries in urban areas, in their hierarchies and recognisable limits, and the radical change in social structure, from stable and consistent to shifting and fluid, have called into question the very nature of traditional urban locations, requiring architecture to experiment constantly. And these changes have also called into question the tools traditionally used for shaping new public spaces.

Added to this is another factor that makes the task even more complex: the stratified relationship with the many stories and traditions that continue to brand our territory, raising the subtle issue of the identity of places and individuals, and how to interpret that in contemporary terms, without any mawkish melancholy or dangerous neo-Romantic tendencies.

When I sat down and calmly observed Ifdesign's designs for the black and white town squares in Robbiano, it struck me just what a tough task new Italian architecture has been called upon to fulfil, and what a wonderful opportunity we have to be around at such a difficult yet challenging time.

The issue is elementary: to rethink the space given over to the parvis in front of San Quirico and Santa Giulitta, two churches placed in parallel and separated by a road on the outskirts of the town.

The choice seems natural, almost dictated by common sense: to extend the parvis – that vestibular space between the two churches – thus restoring a unity which had been lost.

Yet from this point on, things became even more interesting.

Two churches, two parvis, two colours which maintain the hierarchy between the two spaces. White in front of the main church, black for the Collegiate Church. It was more than just a question of deciding on the materials: it was about establishing and resolving boundaries with discreet but sophisticated clarity.

The stone blocks are treated with a functional decorative pattern which transforms the parvis into a soft carpet paving the space, clearly delineating the boundaries (think of the multitude of Madonnas Enthroned in 15th century European painting and the masterful use of Oriental fabrics as floor-coverings. In the transition from day to night, the street is covered with black basalt, treated with the cipher of the automobile tyre. And the black town square runs downhill from the Collegiate Church, turning into a cosy geological fold, a welcoming bench turning its back on a fountain with its subtle sound of running water.

This little project for a village square teaches us about the need to think up public places which offer the comforts of a welcoming home, the simplicity of a timeless design, and the strength and generosity required to welcome anyone, offering them a dilated concept of time, so that they can fulfil their need for reconciliation between places and everyday life.

Luca Molinari, Milano-based architecture critic.

General plan

Paving detail

In the centre of Robbiano, the San Quirico and Giulitta churches once looked on to a widened section of Via Battisti that was both of ambiguous identity and poorly related with the remaining urban fabric. The town council decided to make this area meaningful and worthy of being the main square. The two churches gave rise to the idea of treating it as a vestibular space notable for its dualism. The difference in height – some 3 metres – between the churches and Via Battisti also had to be resolved.

The project takes the form of two regular carpet-like areas in front of each church, floating on a homogenous background of granite blocks. With their contrasting chromatic valences, the carpets are strict opposites. The one in front of the Giulitta Church is black and paved in basalt. It leads up to the church door and includes two basalt-block benches separating the church from a pool of water with a small fountain. The San Quirico carpet is paved in white Trani stone, dropping down from the level of the church and generating a large flight of steps. At the lower level, it flattens into a small platform before folding back on itself to form a bench. The scale is monumental, with the idea of providing an apt setting for weddings, funerals and processions. The stairway is ideal for group photographs with the church as background, while the bottom platform can be used for parking a bridal car or hearse.

The minimalist simplicity of the intervention does not ignore the need to bestow meaning on the place before turning it into the town square. The dualism of the two contrasting carpets creates a dynamising polarity, transforming the former featurelessness into a public space that is at once symbolic and clearly functional.

PROJECT **Piazza Nera Piazza Bianca (Black Square White Square), Robbiano, Italy**
DATE **2005**
AUTHORS **Ifdesign: Franco Tagliabue Volontè, Chiara Toscani, Ida Origgi**
DEVELOPER **Commune di Giussano**
SURFACE **2,500 m²**
COST **317,000 €**

Krakow

Heroes of the Ghetto Square

PIOTR LEWICKI & KAZIMIERZ ŁATAK

[SPECIAL MENTION]
2006

Empty Chairs
ADAM ZAGAJEWSKI

This is a rather small square. Nothing grandiose about it. Seventy years ago there were little houses around it (nowadays there are some accents of the city's development nearby) – but even now the overall impression is provincial, it could almost be a small town somewhere near the mountains, one of the shtetls that were once so numerous in the Polish Galicia. The city of Krakow with its huge churches, majestic main square and royal castle seems to be far away – the center of the city is across the river, Wisla or Vistula, which according to Oswald Spengler, the author of *The Decline of the West* – a great stylist but not a very great historian – marked the boundary between Europe and Asia. So if Nazis were well read they expelled the Krakow Jews from Europe to Asia (they created the ghetto on the south bank of the river, Jews were driven out from their dwelling places in the other city districts).

Krakow used to be an important Jewish city, a place where learned rabbis had taught who attracted students from other towns and countries. Two years ago at the march which every third Sunday in March commemorates the expulsion of the Jews from the north bank – especially from Kazimierz which was home for many of them – and the creation of a ghetto near the square in question, I met a man from Israel, an MD, who told me and other people, other friends, that his family had lived in Krakow for 500 years. He pronounced these words with a kind of sensual pleasure: 500 years! He spoke as if feeling under his tongue the detailed, varied history of all these years, one after another. Five centuries, some of them peaceful, some filled with wars and catastrophes. And this half of a millennium ended here, at the square which earlier was called Plac Zgody (Concord Square) and now bears the name of Bohaterów Getta (Heroes of the Ghetto).

If you see the square for the first time, you might ask: what are these chairs doing here? These chairs are not provincial, they are bigger than the usual ones, the 'real' ones, they are almost like thrones in a strange monarchy where there would be 33 kings. The kings are absent though, the thrones are empty. They are embedded in the pavement and exposed to the slow procession of the seasons year; right now, in late January, they are covered by snow. Before the refurbishing of the square this particular part of the city was a sort of the seasons of the year; nondescript place: a streetcar stop would produce plenty of people from the suburbs rushing to the city or, in the late afternoon, returning to their semi-rural housings. There would be probably a few fruit and vegetable stands as well; an uninteresting urban patch which one would rather avoid, heading instead for more meaningful spots. Also this kind of a rather low life that was taking place here was somehow the very opposite of memory. It was oblivious and formless. When you have around you booths selling vegetables and fruit it's certainly good for your diet but not so good for the memory; vegetables famously have none...

The presence of the chairs has changed everything here. The emptiness of the chairs triggers thinking. It's a negative monument, so much more powerful than a possible banal depiction of the victims of the tragedy. The emptiness invites our imagination. The chairs allude also, it seems, to a not so new fashion of modern monuments where you'd see a writer, an artist, a well-known scientist, a social activist represented as a low-key statue; a bench or a chair with a human figure, reading or smoking a pipe or just meditating. Never on a pedestal but near the viewer, at street level, at eye level. The chairs in the square are like this except that there are no human figures here. No human figures: the potential sitters, potential monument-heroes were gone for ever before they could have become what they were destined for. The emptiness of the chairs is more telling than the possible human figures...

The square has become a noble place now. The chessboard of the chairs is structuring the space, giving it a distinct pattern. The square is thinking.

Adam Zagajewski, Krakow-based poet and writer.

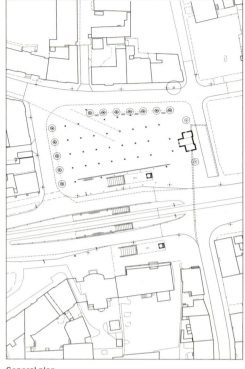

General plan

The former Plac Zgody (Concord Square) was designated by the Nazis as the Umschlagplatz (assembly point) where Jews had to gather before deportation. In 1943, once the Krakow ghetto was emptied, the belongings they had to leave behind before starting their last journey to Auschwitz or Plaszow were piled up here. Sixty years later, the only sign of this dreadful past was its change of name to Plac

Bohaterów Getta (Ghetto Heroes Square). The council then decided to refurbish the square in homage to the victims. Instead of installing a single monument that would speak literally of the tragedy, they used the square itself to convey memory. A grid of chairs has been fixed on slightly raised platforms over a spread of paving in grey syenite rock so that they appear to be floating, with a

dreamlike air that is heightened after a snowfall when their darkness stands out against the abstract whiteness of the snow. The chairs and other objects in the square are made of bronze or rust-coloured wrought iron. Waste-paper bins, tram stop shelters, bicycle parks and even traffic signs, stripped of their usual functionalism, acquire a symbolic character to evoke the memory of the Jews' belongings abandoned in the Umschlagplatz. Paradoxically, in the Plac Bohaterów Getta, the memory of tremendous events is summoned up through ordinary objects. The distance normally separating street furniture from monuments is blurred here in a surprising reconciliation between function and symbolism. Shunning sublimation of the tragedy, this contained intervention admits ordinary everyday use of the square without eluding the responsibility of making the presence of all the absent strongly felt.

PROJECT **Heroes of the Ghetto Square, Krakow, Poland**
DATE **2005**
AUTHORS **Piotr Lewicki & Kazimierz Łatak**
DEVELOPER **City of Krakow**
SURFACE **13,093 m²**
COST **3,000,000 €**

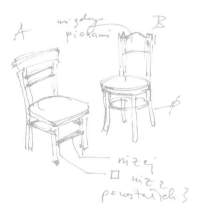

Volkspalast

[SPECIAL PRIZE OF THE JURY]
2006

German Houses
DIRK LAUCKE

Peace to the Hovels! Death to the Palaces!
Georg Büchner

May 8, 2005. Somewhere behind me, at the Brandenburg Gate, the 'Celebration of Democracy' rages. And just like every other form of rule in Germany, the people celebrate democracy with beer and bratwurst. A glass wall stands before me. I look out onto Alexanderplatz and knock furiously on the window. If the glass wasn't in the way, and if I could spit 50 meters, then I could hit one of the Nazis demonstrating in the plaza. I'm standing in the Palast der Republik, the Palace of the Republic. Absent are the flooded hallways and the rubber-boat tours, very popular with the tourists, and so is the scaffolding installation representing a mountain. Somehow, the whole thing is empty. And I realize that I have somehow managed, just following the crowds, to trespass in this historic place, soon to be a mere relic of the past. As I begin to look around, I ascend to one of the upper floors, out onto a kind of balcony, where I can at least yell down at the marching Nazis: «West or East, down with the Nazi beast!» Right above my head, the only sign of modern art in the Volkspalast: ZWEIFEL (doubt), written by the artist Lars Ramberg. At least something that the Nazis will see for sure, at least I think. The first groups of police officers begin to arrive in their black armor, and the cry of the first protestor that gets sight of them is the start signal for the flight from the rain of police batons. I leave the Volkspalast, rejoin the crowds, a bratwurst in one hand and a German flag in the other.

It was the 60th anniversary of the end of the Second World War. In case you've forgotten, the war was started by invading Germans and was much more than a war. What's more, the Germans had been living for 14 years in an enlarged, reunited Germany.

But unlike the gargantuan Olympic Stadium and Tempelhof Airport, both from the architectural offices of Hitler&Speer, and both of which dominate and mar the atmosphere of Berlin, the Palast der Republik, the model construction of the GDR, was to give way to the wrecking ball. Perhaps the demolition confirmed the Western war-victors' notion that East German Socialism was nothing but a ridiculous attempt by old men with funny glasses to lead an alternative, more economically just society. (If you ask me, this attempt not only landed on its face, but also broadsided all those forced to live and die in that experiment.) Perhaps the demolition of the Palast and the continued existence of Hitler's buildings, as well as the planned restoration of the Prussian Stadtschloss (City Palace), only confirm that Germans coped with their history then as they do now – without a hint of criticism.

Even before the Palast der Republik became a temporary zone of artistic development, it was always a place for performances. It served the staging of power, the presentation of the state council and SED party conventions, just as it served to present the friendly harmlessness of the GDR with folk TV and concerts. After the fall of the GDR and the collapse of the other Socialist countries, the building's purpose was gone, and the heaps of asbestos within the walls were a kind of representation of the cancerous body of the aging Eastern bloc. At some point, it had to die. Yet the death of Socialism and the sweeping victory of capitalism in just about every corner of the globe seemed to provide the definitive evidence that the 'utopia' once celebrated by the European left was gone for good. It vanished along with the living circumstances of many former citizens of the GDR, for many of whom only the bitterness of being unfairly on the losing side remained. In 2005, the 'Friends of the Palast' mobilized against the 'campaign of organized destruction' they regarded as being based on flimsy arguments. And they even managed to cast themselves in the same light as the victims of National Socialism. In case you've forgotten, the term 'campaign of destruction' primarily stands for the ruthless plundering, deportations, forced labor and mass executions that the Wehrmacht and the SS carried out against civilians on the Eastern front, driven by racist and anti-Semitic motives.

Even their opponents, the restorers of the façade of the Stadtschloss and the protagonists of the 'Humboldt Forum' invoked the Second World War and its victims for their argument. This time, however, German architecture was the victim. Allied bombing campaigns had destroyed the greater part of the old architecture in the center of Berlin, which was then replaced with unattractive modern buildings. And the «gap arising from the bombing of the Schloss must be filled» (Initiative Berliner Stadtschloss). The Palast der Republik was not, therefore, regarded as a symbol of a sunken Socialist system, but as a «gap.» Presumably, the reconstruction and the 'rehabilitation

One of East Germany's most important buildings, the Palast der Republik was constructed in 1976 over the foundations of the Berliner Stadtschloss, a baroque castle previously demolished by the GDR authorities as a symbol of Prussian imperialism. Besides the parliament and the Socialist Unity Party meeting hall, the palace housed a theatre, exhibition hall, restaurant, café and ice cream parlour, discotheque and a bowling alley. After asbestos fibres were detected a month before reunification, it was dismantled leaving only the structure, which was very costly to demolish owing to its proximity to the cathedral. In 2003, the Bundestag decided to replace the palace with a park until finding sufficient funds for the Humboldt Forum, a building planned with a museum and library, and baroque facades imitating the old Berliner Stadtschloss.

The project was controversial. Some people wanted no reminder of the architecture of the fallen regime. Others wanted to conserve

it, arguing that the baroque-style restoration was anachronistic. The Volkspalast platform, formed by the latter, saw the structure as a chance to experiment with a new kind of multifunctional cultural centre. Thanks to this initiative, over 300,000 visitors enjoyed many activities including concerts, art installations, exhibitions and sporting events before its demolition in February 2006, even though funding for the Humboldt Forum had not yet been obtained.

In a city that had been divided for 40 years, the Palast der Republik might have seemed offensive to some but demolishing it meant repeating the error of destroying the Berliner Stadtschloss. The Volkspalast initiative attempted to overcome its controversial connotations and give new meaning to the structure, thus demonstrating that by transforming the uses of a building it is possible to neutralise its symbolic charge and preserve it for the future as an inoffensive witness to a history that cannot be erased.

PROJECT **Volkspalast, Berlin, Germany**
DATE **2005**
AUTHORS
ZwischenPalastNutzung
DEVELOPER **Sophiensäle, HAU**
SURFACE **60,000 m²**
COST **600,000 €**

of Berlin Mitte' (Berliner Stadtschloss Development Association) aimed to fill an historical gap that appears primarily as an act of ignoring or avoiding questions. A gap that could have been closed would have related to Germany between 1933 and 1990. With the reconstruction of the baroque façade of the Stadtschloss, the planners and the German Parliament worked toward an aesthetic touristic attraction, in which «the grandiose European culture would be intertwined with the American way of life and the pep of Berlin.» There are those who criticize that the Stadtschloss also stands for the continuity of the Prussian military tradition, while the planners talk of sales numbers and perhaps confirm the view of those who claim that utopias are gone forever.

And the alliance for the Palast der Republik, which partly emerged from the project of the Volkspalast, «stands for a new generation, wholly detached from the ideological debate of 'Palast or Schloss', that wants to focus on the doable.» The alliance's critique primarily concerned cost issues and the preservation of existing architecture in a city belonging to those who live there. It was thus that the Volkspalast gave life to the ruins with various artistic projects and offered at least some free space for a discourse on the city and its historical roots. The very fact that the 'Palast' was taken control of by people who – without notable commercial ambitions – were actively involved in the shaping of their city speaks for itself. After all, the job of palaces is to have their own doors knocked down and to lose the representation of a dominating elite. History teaches that this can be but temporary.

I must admit that in 2005, I was initially unaffected by Ramberg's *ZWEIFEL* when I drove by the Palast der Republik or saw it in the press. Yet, on the 8th May, as I found myself – literally! – between German citizens celebrating democracy and German Nazis lamenting the loss of their heroes, I either began to become paranoid or to grasp the undeniable ideology of buildings. That ideology can only be shattered by occupying them, as in the brief attempt undertaken by the project Volkspalast – the name has begun to annoy me, but I'll ignore that for a moment. And I ask myself: Is it just an irony of history, or symbolic, that the steel of what was once the paragon of Socialist architecture found its last use in the engines of the NS-founded company VOLKSwagen?

Dirk Laucke, Berlin-based playwright.

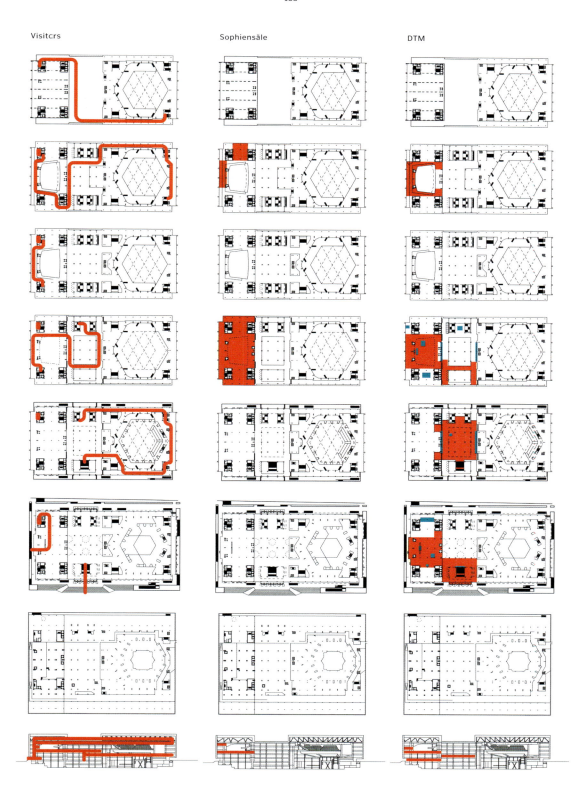

Temporary occupations

2004

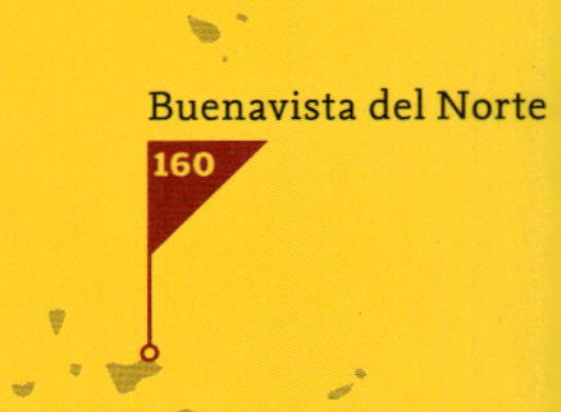

Buenavista del Norte
160

Begues

Restoration of the Vall d'en Joan Controlled Landfill Site

BATLLE I ROIG ARQUITECTES + TERESA GALÍ-IZARD

[JOINT WINNER]
2004

A Mountain of Refuse
JOAN NOGUÉ

In the Garraf Massif and right in the middle of a natural park of metropolitan vocation, the Vall d'en Joan was nothing other than a mountain of refuse. Here we have a paradigm of mass production and the consumer society that is capable even of covering itself with its own rubbish. Human beings have always generated waste: the novelty of the last two centuries has been their inability to recycle it, absorb it and the prodigious volume it has acquired, to the point that it is modelling and becoming part of the landscape, which is what has happened in the case that concerns us here.

In effect, this is a mountain of rubbish some 80 metres high, which is precisely the original depth of the Vall d'en Joan ravine. Life's paradoxes. It happens that the mountain has, in many cultures, been a mythical space *par excellence*. It has had, and still has, an exceptional spiritual and symbolic dimension, and this is particularly the case in Catalonia. The mountain has been a point of generation and irradiation of myths, legends and fables, a centre of meanings, a space of initiation, a supposedly 'virgin', 'pristine' element of the landscape in which even the origins of collective identity have been sought. Years, centuries, have gone by yet, in good measure, we continue imbibing today from the same aesthetic sources that imbued the mountain with this peculiar halo.

The landscape restoration project of the huge 85-hectare controlled landfill site in the Vall d'en Joan, where most of the urban waste of Barcelona and its metropolitan area used to end up, has many virtues. I would highlight, even more than the successful intervention and the transformation of a foul, dismal place into a public space, its symbolic dimension since it has succeeded in returning 'the place to the place' (forgive the repetition) through landscape recycling that has been carried out in a space which is probably the most appropriate one of all when it comes to talking about recycling: a landfill site. The use of local species in the process of re-vegetation, the emulation of the agroforestry mosaics of the most immediate surroundings, the topographic shaping structured into terraces, which are very usual in Mediterranean

mountains, all come together here to return the place to the place. The colossal amount of accumulated rubbish that should have been recycled at its place of origin without ever reaching the Vall d'en Joan, is now recycled *en masse* by means of converting a damaged, depersonalised dump-landscape into a setting for public use and pleasure, and it will also turn out to be socially relevant and even interesting in energy terms, in particular when millions of cubic metres of methane coming from the biogas given off by the fermentation of the rubbish are exported into the power grid without carbon dioxide emissions into the atmosphere.

Fortunately, we are witnessing today many landscape recycling initiatives but it should be admitted that this one is particularly emblematic. I believe that it goes further than the simple restoration that goes with converting damaged terrains into new places of leisure and recreation. There are dozens of cases where old industrial sites have been salvaged and turned into new cultural areas, some of them, in my view, too much in keeping with the sort of thinking that inspires theme parks. The project under discussion here has managed to go one step further and to 'look' in a special way at these neglected, decadent landscapes in order to speak of them as subjects rather than as mere sub-products of the uses that make them marginal; to reconvert them

The Vall d'en Joan was a gully in the Garraf Massif which, in 1974, was designated as the main rubbish dump for the metropolitan area of Barcelona. The waste material that piled up over three decades filled up a large hole of 60 hectares in area and 80 metres deep. Hence the area acquired an artificial topography shaped by terraces, banks and the ramps on which the rubbish trucks moved. Meanwhile, leaching from the tip drained down through the porous ground, releasing methane gas into the atmosphere, this representing 20% of the greenhouse gases given off by the entire city of Barcelona over the same period.
In 1999 a plan was approved for the phased closure of the tip for a time during which educational visits would be organised while the restoration of the landscape was taking place. The latter project envisaged integrating the former rubbish dump, now public space, into the Garraf Natural Park by 2010. The artificial topography was respected and consoli-

dated, while access was organised by means of walls constructed of gabions filled with recycled waste, these evoking the earlier use of the site. After sealing, the gabions were covered with another layer of local plant species and crops of legumes so as to facilitate soil regeneration. The surface water network was isolated from the internal network in order to reduce the leaching flows, which are now collected before they filter into the ground and treated in a water-purifying plant. Rainwater feeds into an irrigation network that encourages the process of reforestation in the park, while a collecting system channels the biogas produced by fermentation of the waste materials into a generating plant that is connected with the general power supply.

Despite the wild nature of the zone, the former infrastructure is indissociable from the metropolitan reality that exploited it for 30 years. When toxicity indicators permit, it will become an open park but, meanwhile, its educational, environmental and energy contributions ensure that its value in terms of public service is indisputable.

PROJECT **Restoration of the Vall d'en Joan Controlled Landfill Site, Begues, Spain**
DATE **2003**
AUTHORS **Enric Batlle, Joan Roig, Teresa Galí-Izard**
DEVELOPER **Entitat Metropolitana de Serveis Hidràulics de l'Àrea Metropolitana de Barcelona - Diputació de Barcelona**
SURFACE **2,000,000 m²**
COST **19,983,652 €**

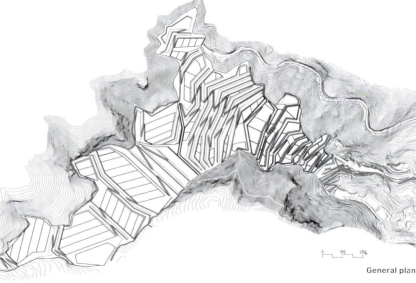

General plan

without thematising them, but rather in the context of a general reconsideration of our relationship with the environment, which needs to change, totally and once and for all, the model that has been standard over the last 200 years.

Shunned landscapes are scattered throughout the territory but they multiply in urban peripheries and in the middle of and next to motorways, main roads and ring routes. We see the landscapes we 'wish' to see, which is to say those that don't challenge our idea of socially constructed places. We seek in landscape those models, those patterns that adapt to the ones we hold in our collective unconscious or those closest to it. This is why these spurned landscapes are invisible to us, even though we see them. One should recall at this point that our everyday geographies are full of unknown landscapes and hidden territories, frequently because of their complex legibility. In my opinion, these typologies of landscape pertaining to advanced capitalist societies should come under a new heading: landscapes of deterioration, of leftovers, of rebuff... in brief, residual landscapes, endowing on the term 'residual' an acceptance that is linked with the residue itself as an object, along with the connotation of something secondary, surplus, superfluous and hence banal, irrelevant, practically invisible.

We tend to associate trash, waste, and leftovers with particular, very common objects of everyday life. If we changed the scale we'd realise that the hegemonic system of production and consumption in the world over the last couple of centuries creates rubbish-spaces that, in turn, shape veritable rubbish-landscapes, and these can be recycled and put to good use. Until we come to concede to these spaces that form residual landscapes a leading role in the territorial project and urban planning interventions, we will be unable to integrate them properly into the new territorial logic. It would mean 'reading' them differently until managing to understand them as active agents and not mute, passive spectators in the territorial and urban planning project. My nose tells me that the authors of this particular project have been able to do just this.

Joan Nogué, professor of Human Geography at the University of Girona and director of the Landscape Observatory of Catalonia.

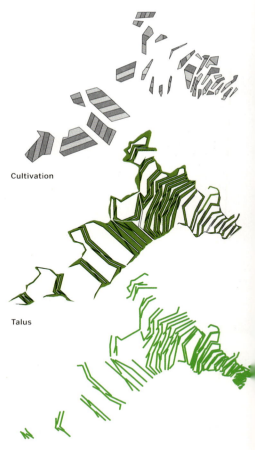

Schemes

Cultivation

Talus

Trees

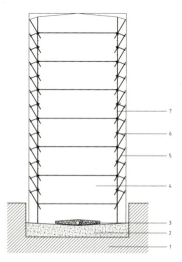

Wall of recycled waste section

Teruel

Refurbishing of the Paseo del Óvalo

DAVID CHIPPERFIELD ARCHITECTS, FERMÍN VÁZQUEZ–B720 ARQUITECTOS

— [JOINT WINNER] —
2004

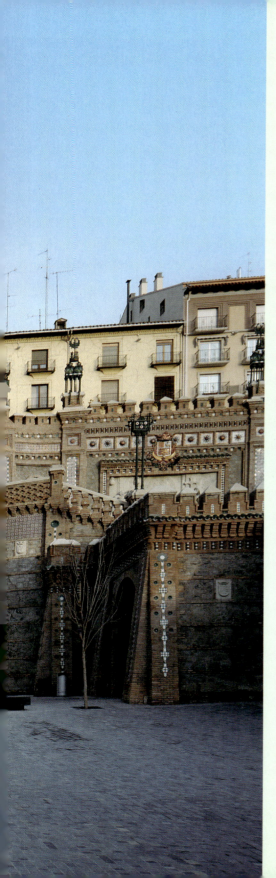

Next Stop, Teruel

LUIS FERNÁNDEZ-GALIANO

Teruel exists, but only at times. It existed with Mudejar splendor in the 13th century, a brief and shining medieval moment that began with a town chapter in 1176 and culminated with the magnificent towers, of the first quarter of the 14th century, which UNESCO has included in its World Heritage list. It existed tragically in the terrible winter of 1937-38 as the scene of one of the Spanish Civil War's most devastating battles, suffering an assault that reduced a good part of the old city to rubble. And it aspires to exist, in this uncertain 21st century, manifesting itself in demands for infrastructure, developing a theme park to expose its paleontological wealth, and summoning leading architects to defend the historic city from the automobile and prepare it for the arrival of the high-speed train.

The Mudejar moment was extraordinarily materialized in the towers, a series of slender brick prisms profusely adorned with geometric filigree and glazed ceramic, whose delicate profiles form part of the old quarter's magical silhouette. Lucky survivors of the brutal battle of Teruel, the Mudejar towers were in the postwar period inserted in an urban landscape efficiently and intelligently reconstructed by the architects of the Devastated Regions program. The city owes them its sober, respectful schemes which, in light of subsequent mistakes, including the chaotic enlargements of the democratic age, must be judged with more respect than irony. Those architects proceeded in the manner of surgical repair, and an obligation to measure up with them has necessarily befallen the teams convoked to refurbish Teruel's west facade: a beautiful cornice over the meadow of the Turia River, crowned by Mudejar towers, that stretches from the seminary to the viaduct, some of whose elements constituted part of the reconstruction of the 1940s and 1950s.

The winner of that competition was the most austere entry, a project by the British architect David Chipperfield with the Barcelona firm Fermín Vázquez/b720. With mannerist sensibility and the skill of an acupuncturist, it perforated the huge retaining wall beside the old Carmelite convent, now the seat of the Aragonese government, to accommodate an elevator construction whose monumental and luminous facade one gets to from the train station by way of a carpet of stone. It highlights the grand neo-Mudejar staircase as if it were a formidable sculpture, pedestrianizes the urban balcony of the Óvalo without altogether obstructing the passage of vehicles, and accommodates under a new tree-adorned roundabout a very efficient parking lot that facilitates access by deterring internal traffic: a painstaking exercise in historic surgery that is quite familiar to an architect who has built simultaneously on Berlin's museum island and on Venice's San Michele island. This first work by Chipperfield was the prologue to a series of urban interventions that are intelligently transforming the historic center, from the remodelling of the Plaza del Torico by the same Fermín Vázquez, with a pavement of luminous needles that are laid out in an at once necessary and haphazard order, to the project for the refurbishment of the Plaza de los Amantes by the Madrid studio of José Ignacio Linazasoro, who proposes an intervention of extreme material sensibility, historical conscience and attention to context, in the sentimental and legendary heart of the city.

The mythical scene of the Mudejar coexistence of Christians and Muslims also staged the dramatic story of the Amantes, driven by adversity and destiny to die of love. The emblematic toponym of the civil conflict's storm of hate was also the venue of a formidable postwar reconstruction process that made it an example of urban renaissance. But the contemporary symbol of marginalization and abandonment only endeavors to tie up seamlessly with that network of flows and places that we call Spain. Teruel has lived its drama of love and its tragedy of hate. It must now play a difficult role in the amiable comedy of a normalized country.

Luis Fernández-Galiano, architect and director of Arquitectura Viva *magazine.*

The old centre of the city of Teruel crowns a promontory that drops sharply with a 17-metre-high containing wall. The Paseo del Óvalo runs around the upper edge offering sweeping views while the railway station square lies at the foot. In the early years of the 20th century, the presence of the railway station was the occasion for constructing a monumental Mudejar-style stairway to connect the two levels. A century later, the coming of the high-speed train meant that it became necessary to restore to this entrance to the city its former representative status.

Both the stairway's structure and its decorative elements were given a meticulous overhaul. A large opening was made in the retaining wall to resemble the gateway in a city wall. The jambs and lintels of this gateway form sloping planes that converge in a rather small square vestibule with a free elevation of 17 metres. To either side are two lifts that go up to the level of the Paseo del Óvalo, leading into it through a glass prism that lets natural light into the vestibule well. In the Paseo del Óvalo, all architectural barriers were eliminated and space was freed to accommodate terraces for small businesses. Benches and street lights have been installed between the trees of the central zone reinforcing the boundary between the circumstantial movement of vehicles and the zone reserved for pedestrians. The traffic restrictions have been complemented with the opening up of alternative routes of access to the old city centre. Present-day requirements of accessibility have made it necessary to achieve the connection between the square and the Paseo del Óvalo by means of mechanical infrastructure. However, beyond merely functional needs, the lifts display a degree of representativeness that has made possible a dignified coexistence with the historic stairway, complementing rather than disturbing its presence.

PROJECT **Refurbishing of the Paseo del Óvalo, Escalinata and surroundings**
DATE **2003**
AUTHORS **David Chipperfield Architects, Fermín Vázquez - b720 Arquitectos**
DEVELOPER **Diputación General de Aragón**
SURFACE **10,048 m²**
COST **6,000,000 €**

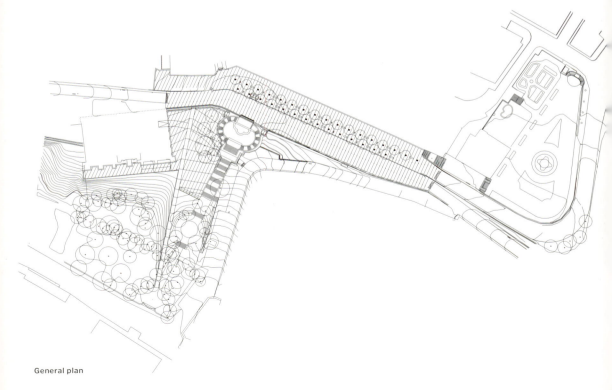

General plan

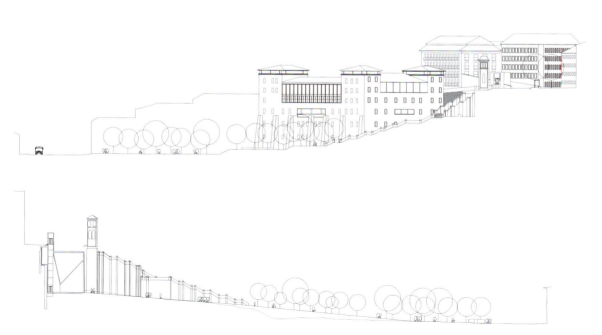

Longitudinal sections

Copenhagen

Harbour Baths

PLOT A/S: BJARKE INGELS & JULIEN DE SMEDT

[SPECIAL MENTION]
2004

Swimming in the City
LARS GEMZØE

The playful design of the swimming bath greatly improved the possibilities for all user groups to enjoy Copenhagen in a new, fresh and different manner. Designed by Plot A/S and located in the Islands Brygge Waterfront Park, the baths are in the harbour close to the city centre. The district is one of the most densely built-up quarters in Copenhagen with many six-storey residential buildings and almost no spaces for recreation. The Islands Brygge area dates from the beginning of the 1900s. There were no parks in the district, which has very narrow courtyards with little potential for outdoor activity. Actually, the streets are wider than the courtyards.

When the commercial and industrial harbour-related activities that had always formed a barrier between the water and the residential area began losing their importance, a grassroots group lobbied for a park on the site instead. The park is only there because the local citizens organized an action committee to prevent this new vacant area from being built upon and to safeguard it as a new park.

In 1978 the group presented a project and in 1983 the Harbour Authority finally granted them the use of the space. Hundreds of the residents planted trees, sowed grass and raised funds to convert the area into a park, piece by piece, and the first simple version of the park was opened in 1984. The head of the action group, architect Poul Jensen and his wife, landscape architect Annelise Bramsnæs, made a plan in 1994, which was the basis for the existing design of the many different attractions on this narrow stretch of land between the city district and the water's edge. The park has new architectural elements, which are supporting different activities mixed with old elements recycled from the old harbour activities tied together by lines of trees and green lawns. The railroad tracks with a single goods-train car and part of the structures from the cranes and the old industrial buildings have been recycled.

The participation of the local citizens is of significant importance, not only because the park is rooted in the neighbourhood, but it also means that the design is based on the local needs and not on a planning operation from the top down.

Today the park has many different areas with different characteristics and broad appeal to many kinds of users and age groups. Functions overlap and nothing is left in isolation. A walk along the water provides the added value of expansive views over the water as well as a glimpse of multifarious activities for spectators and participants alike. Old and young, families, singles and everyone is welcome here.

Once the water in the harbour was clean enough to swim in for the first time since the 1950s, the park added another aquatic element in 2002, a floating harbour swimming baths. After the first season the facility had to be expanded and a new one, designed by the young architects office PLOT/Bjarke Ingels and Julien De Smedt, opened in 2003.

This new version of the swimming baths widely expanded the possibilities for beach life into the middle of the city and quickly became a popular destination. It changed the place from a local park to an exciting hotspot for the whole Copenhagen region. The new design was far more useful and exciting than the simple swimming facility it replaced. It is also more inviting for many more people as even families with small children can use it. The basis for that success is, of course, to a high extent, the new possibility to swim right in the middle of town, but it is also the previous layers of the park, which are part of the background for the success in broader terms as the park has a lot more to offer than swimming.

The area attracts a widely varied section of the city's residents regardless of gender, skin colour and age, and on a sunny summer day an average of 1,000 people can be found enjoying the park throughout the day and well into the evening.

Lars Gemzøe, architect, associated partner in Gehl Architects APS, Copenhagen.

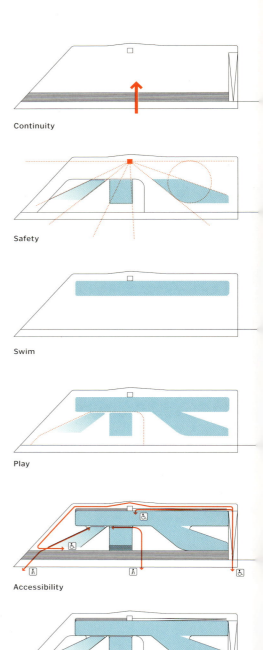

Diagrams

Continuity

Safety

Swim

Play

Accessibility

Harbourscape

Around the middle of the 20th century, the Islands Brygge neighbourhood ceased to be a placid place looking on to the canal and became an industrial sector. By 1954 water pollution led to the closing of the popular Rysensteen public baths and the neighbourhood became progressively marginal. Recently, however, it has undergone a thorough transformation which has entailed the replacement of the factories by new residential buildings and the creation of Havneparken, a park consisting of three large parterres of grass extending like a beach along the 250 metres of the quay.
In 2003, the council promoted the construction of the Havnebadet, or Harbour Baths, a long platform running along the canal in juxtaposition to the central part of the Havneparken. Rectangular in shape and 25 metres wide by 90 metres long, the construction has a surface of wooden planks that is interrupted to make space for four swimming pools of different forms and sizes. A 4-metre-high block of wood, in the form of a ship's prow functions as a diving board while a watchtower reminiscent of a ship's funnel has an uninterrupted view over the whole site. A pergola has been constructed with the steel beams recovered from one of the demolished factories, while the upside-down hull of a ferry acts as the roof of a drinks kiosk. With islands of water on an island of earth, the Harbour Baths offer swimmers good access and salubrious, secure conditions. The neighbourhood has thereby recovered its former popularity of the days of the Rysensteen baths. However, shunning nostalgic revisionism, this journey to better times has been undertaken from an optimistic standpoint that offers innovative ways of bathing, while also employing a rich repertoire of formal elements that testify to the industrial past of the neighbourhood.

PROJECT **Harbour Baths, Copenhagen, Denmark**
DATE **2003**
AUTHORS **PLOT A/S: Bjarke Ingels & Julien De Smedt**
PARTICIPANTS **CC DESIGN, Birch & Krogboe**
DEVELOPER **Municipality of Copenhagen**
SURFACE **2,500 m²**
COST **580,000 €**

Berlin's Voids

ANDREAS HUYSSEN

It takes Berlin – a city famous for its green areas, broad boulevards, and empty urban spaces – to prize a rectangular park consisting only of grassy unplanted surfaces and lined by two parallel streets with a row of linden trees on each side. The Tilla Durieux Park fills an extended narrow esplanade of open space (500 x 75 metres), left by the railway tracks of the former Potsdamer Bahnhof and now framed by the rather uniformly structured building façades of identical height on either side. Upon entering the park at Potsdamer Platz, your gaze hits upon a strange 4 metre-high elevation that rises steeply on one side and slopes gently down on the other to form a kind of grassy beach toward the Potsdamer Platz area. A prize-winning landscaping project, the Tilla Durieux Park opened in 2003, forming an ensemble with other urban green spaces the city of Berlin has been developing since unification. Its central feature is a voluminous turf and grass sculpture consisting of two longitudinal slightly contorted parterres. A paved transversal passage displaying four unfathomably longish seasaws crosses in between and connects the Renzo Piano and Richard Rogers buildings on one side with Grassi's monotonous ABB housing and office complexes across the way. Significantly, the highest segment of the grassy surface conjures up memories of the Wall. It ran right here in the same direction, before sharply turning eastward toward Stresemannstrasse and Checkpoint Charlie. Indeed, there is something slightly oppressive about the whole geometric structure, accentuated no doubt by the absence of bushes, flowers, and trees. At the same time the robust volume of the two parterres resonates with the massive and largely uniform façades of the buildings on either side. In that sense the architects captured the imaginary of this central post-unification space quite successfully.

The pervasive emptiness of the space, intensely palpable in the snowy wintery darkness of Berlin, conjures up other images and memories of Berlin's voids – images of Wenders's *Himmel über Berlin* from before 1989, some of it filmed in this very area, and memories of the alternative squatters' settlement during the post-89 transition and the Polish black market in the years thereafter. While the void between Brandenburg Gate and Potsdamer Platz has now been filled with new construction including the American Embassy and the Eisenmann Memorial to the Murdered Jews of Europe, the Tilla Durieux Park is the only public void left in an area that once marked the threshold between the Imperial city and the bourgeois west, and later the divide between East and West Berlin. But unlike that earlier post-89 void in the center of Berlin, created by the dismantling of the Wall and saturated by memories of the ruins of history (Reichskanzlei, Hitler's bunker, Speer's plans for the North-South axis, and later the Wall's minefields), the Tilla-Durieux Park is a void ultimately without history. It does resonate, however, with what many Berliners have described as the new sense of emptiness that characterizes the reconstructed Potzdamer Platz area itself – a lifeless tourist attraction advertising itself with fancy names such as Marlene Dietrich Platz and Tilla-Durieux Park, but avoided by most Berliners and now also abandoned by some of its most prestigious business occupants such as Daimler Chrysler and Sony. The signature of this whole area is not the desired urban density, but urban emptiness – despite its success with the throngs of tourists who lounge on the grassy slopes of the park during the summer devouring their fast food and feigning relaxation.

To me, the surface emptiness of the park resonates with what Siegfried Kracauer captured so well in his urban sketches of the 1920s, short prose texts about Paris, Marseilles and Berlin, all critical of the draining of life from an older urban fabric in the process of modernization. The Tilla Durieux Park together with Potsdamer Platz today may be the contemporary equivalent for what Kracauer, astute observer and fierce critic of urban modernity, labeled «natural geometry» – an abstract schema stamped on urban and civil life that has nothing natural about it. A voided void paradigmatic of an ambitious reconstruction gone awry.

Andreas Huyssen, Villard Professor of German and Comparative Literature, Columbia University, New York.

When the Berlin Wall came down, many spaces of the bare strip of land that went with it acquired new strategic prominence. Such is the case of the Prachtgleis, an esplanade, 500 metres long and 75 metres wide, next to Potsdamer Platz. Most of the empty spaces surrounding the square were filled up during the heyday of construction in the 1990s but the Prachtgleis was left as a markedly delimited strip between two rows of residential and tertiary buildings, a large, cut-off, undeveloped yawning gap.

In 1995, the city council called for entries in an international competition to create a green zone with a view to mitigating the density of the neighbourhood. The result is the Tilla Durieux Park, which consists of two large parterres of grass, each one 30 metres wide and 200 metres long, running in a longitudinal direction. Like two green beaches facing away from one another, the parterres have gentle transversal slopes running

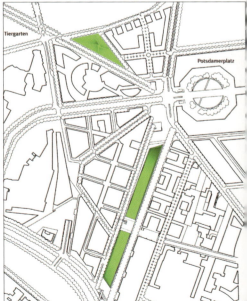

Plan

in opposite directions. The slopes rise to more than 4 metres above street level, dropping then to form a rather more steeply-angled bank. They are outlined in the longitudinal direction by two rows of linden trees separating them from the traffic in the two streets at the perimeters. The two strips are separated by a paved space that provides a route through the park to the Marlene Dietrich Platz, this thoroughfare area being equipped with five 20-metre-long metal seesaws. Given the intensity of the stylistic and formal variations of the surrounding architecture, the soothing, expressive minimalism of Tilla Durieux Park offers a yearned-for breathing space. Inside a huge constructed mass it shapes a majestic exception that bestows on the centre of Berlin a green beach that is enjoyed by many people. In this idyllic celebration of emptiness there is some hint of reference to the Wall so that it is still present in its absence.

PROJECT **Tilla Durieux Park, Berlin, Germany**
DATE **2003**
AUTHORS **DS Landschapsarchitecten, Maike van Stiphout, Jana Crepon, Harma Horlings, Bruno Doedens, Ingo Golz, Merijn Groenhart, Willem Jan Snel**
PARTICIPANTS **Carolien Oomes, Thomas Dietrich**
DEVELOPER **Stadsdeel Mitte, Berlin**
SURFACE: **2,250,000 m²**
COST **2,250,000 €**

Conceptual sketch

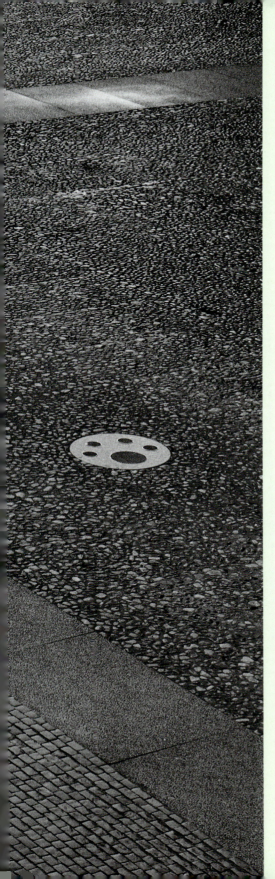

Living Archaeology
PHILIP URSPRUNG

Field stones of various shapes and colours which were smoothed by glaciers during hundreds of thousands of years belong to the many remnants of the last ice age in the Baltic area. Anyone who has visited North-Eastern Germany, Poland, or Sweden, will remember the beauty of these stones and recall the tactile sensation of walking over the uneven surfaces that they form. Since medieval times these field stones were used as building materials for churches, walls, and houses, for roads and town-squares. A particularly impressive square made out of field stones can be found in the centre of the Swedish town Kalmar. The Stortorget – Swedish for 'main square' – goes back to the early 18th century. It was modified in the 1920s with cut granite stones to differentiate pedestrian and vehicle areas and was, until recently, used as a parking place.

In the late 1990s the authorities of Kalmar intended to rebrand the city centre by revamping their Stortorget. Caruso St John in collaboration with the Swedish artist Eva Löfdahl won the international competition arranged by the Swedish Arts Council in 1999. Their proposal was both simple and highly conceptual. They basically removed what was not necessary. They reconfigured the whole square and arranged it according to patterns. They removed the granite flagstones and kerbstones that had been added in the 1920s as well as some of the field stones. Sixty percent of the field stones remained in situ and were simply cleaned slightly. New, regularly cut stones were added. Besides the stones, the architects inserted new paths of precast concrete coated with a layer of pebbles, which correspond to the field stones. These are more comfortable to walk on, and stand in contrast to the patina of the material collected in the fields and excavated in quarries centuries ago. Furthermore, the architects introduced wells and light poles that define a subterranean acoustic spatiality and a virtual air space.

Caruso St John erased all physical traces of history, namely the unevenness and dirt left by cars during the last decades. They retained the beauty and dignity of the old material but refused the usual gesture in historical reconstruction which is popular all around Europe, namely to frame or stage the vestiges of the past, to keep them visible like fetishes or trophies. This gesture is the consequence of an ahistorical and acultural perspective, in the sense that it focuses on sheer materiality. By eliminating traces of change, by insisting on an original state, they prevent and separate the past from the present and therefore assist in the commodification of public space. Since the 1990s, major parts of old cities like Berlin, Dresden and Barcelona, but also smaller towns in northern Italy, Scandinavia and Austria thus virtually have been turned into theme parks.

Caruso St John are very well aware of this problem. Instead of conserving a palimpsest of 'authentic' material and producing phantasmatic images of local identity, which can easily be exploited by the tourism industry, they designed a contingent, depthless composition. The old that had been crushed by the new is not evoked as a nostalgic image, but becomes inseparably intertwined with the new. The result is a surface that literally opens the public sphere. The arrangement could, theoretically, be changed again. Its meaning is not fixed. But it also resists instrumentalization. Rather than giving in to the pressure of commercial use and historical reconstruction, Stortorget is a statement for the autonomy, beauty and fragility of both architecture and the public sphere.

Philip Ursprung is Professor of Modern and Compory Art at the University of Zürich.

A city-centre square expressing political, religious and military power, Stortorget is 90 metres wide and 110 metres long and surrounds Kalmar's baroque cathedral. A good part of the city's history is stored in its 300-year-old paving. It consists of the same rough-hewn stones that were used in the past to construct dry-stone walls for marking off fields, building the walls of houses and paving the streets throughout the city. Yet the rich variety of grain, colour and texture of these stones contrasted with the homogeneity of the granite slabs and borders. The latter were subsequently added to mark out, on the square, tracks for the cars that haphazardly used the space as a parking lot until 2003. The renovation of Stortorget did not arise so much from the urgent need to improve its state of conservation as from the wish to restore the dignity it had lost with this intervention. Removed with a view to reusing them in other parts of the city, the granite flagstones have been replaced by cobblestones that restore the square's continuity. The new sections were finished with touches that distinguish them from the original stones, thus forming a patchwork pattern that is reminiscent of marquetry work. Some gaps are filled with matching rounded pieces and some with slabs of prefabricated concrete incrusted with small granite pebbles. In order to relieve the orthogonality of the layout, several round pieces with small circular grilles – through which one can hear the sound of underground water circulating through a series of interconnected wells – have been set into the surface at different points. Stortorget regained its lost dignity when it was stripped of superfluous elements and restored to its original state which was characterised by sober emptiness. At the same time, the delicate pattern of pieces that completes the original paving makes this sobriety feel more welcoming, while also differing from the pre-existing paving thanks to a contemporary but harmonious solution that shuns the conceptual impertinence and technical complications of a mimetic solution.

PROJECT **Stortorget, Kalmar, Sweden**
DATE **2003**
AUTHORS **Caruso St John Architects, Adam Caruso, Peter St. John, Eva Löfdahl**
CLIENT **Kalmar Kommum, Statens Konstråd**
SURFACE **14,000 m²**
COST **840,000 €**

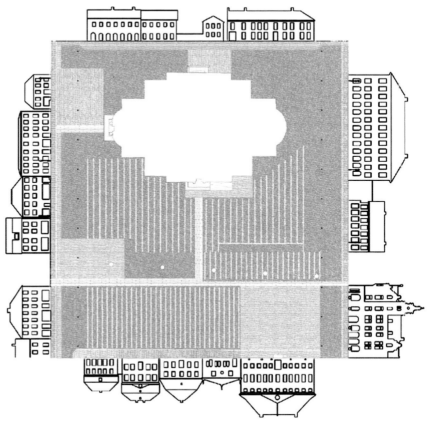

General plan

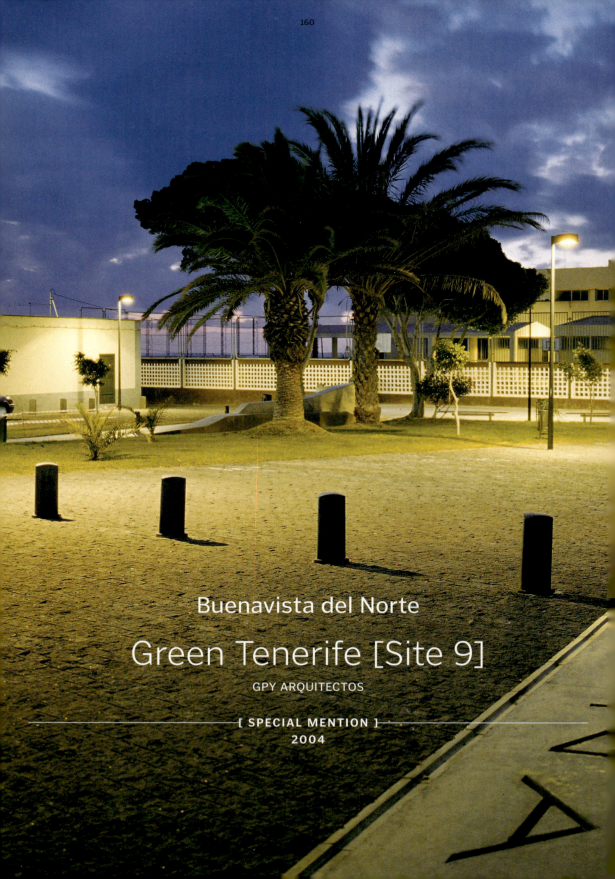

Buenavista del Norte

Green Tenerife [Site 9]

GPY ARQUITECTOS

[SPECIAL MENTION]
2004

Coexistence and Interaction

MARINA ROMERO

If there is anything that particularly attracts one's attention in small towns like Buenavista del Norte with its scant 6,000 inhabitants, it is how public spaces become settings in which the daily life of the townspeople takes place and how people tend to take over such collective space.

If the value of public space lies, along with its other qualities, in its capacity for generating social interaction, Buenavista also reveals some ambivalence, which may be common to rural settlements. It generates interaction because this is where people come together to chat, play, watch processions, and attend carnival and pilgrimage festivities but if, as Jordi Borja remarks, «it could be assessed, among other factors, for its power to mingle groups», this is not the case here. For example, the older people gather every afternoon to while away the hours with board games in the Plaza de los Remedios, the original town centre, in front of the church. The Plaza de Triana, which has been redesigned by GPY Arquitectos, is where the children come to play after school, 'taking' the bench-sculpture while their mothers wait in the lookout with its views over the ravine. In the Plaza del Chorro, a group of young people comes together every day to play cards, taking over the square almost exclusively since, in the absence of street furniture, they have taken matters into their own hands and constructed a table and some benches with planks of wood. Hence the square has become a meeting place, but what makes it special is that these young people consider it theirs because they have equipped it themselves and they are the only ones who use it. Another case is the design of the Parque de San Francisco, which includes the already existing sports complex grounds and an old convent. Here, the architects planned a pavilion as a revitalising element in order, as the report states, to «complement the sports-leisure uses of the park». This construction on the edge of the park was used as a Youth House and one of its corners was turned into a drinks stand for festive occasions. Owing to several ruckuses involving the town's young people, it was closed down for years because of the apparent inertia of the local council when it came to finding solutions or alternatives. What was meant to be a surface that would unfold and open out to become part of the park became a background for graffiti. However, what the construction has not lost is its role in constituting the limit between the square and the street, as well as providing refuge beneath the projecting roof that, in turn, gives access to this space.

The Parque de San Francisco, like the rest of the intervention, has been constructed with few means and materials. The paths are shaped by bits of leftover local stone extracted *ex profeso* for the rehabilitation of the Buenavista Church, while spatial complexity has been achieved with a series of small infrastructural elements – walls, taluses, steps, pavements and ramps.

The complexity of the geometries, which is characteristic of the projects of these architects, has managed to minimalise the visual impact of the pre-existing sports complex, which is hidden behind the taluses and vegetation. It also means that while some people are using the field for sporting activities, others can meet on the steps, stroll along the paths, or play on the grass around the old convent. The value of the team's intervention in Buenavista de Norte is to be found in the fact of its having achieved coexistence between traditional spaces – like the Plaza de los Remedios – and the newly designed ones. They have managed to interweave by means of pedestrian pathways a new urban network that maintains the spatial relations between the recent innovations and what previously existed – an approach that is very different from that of wiping the slate clean – so that memory can endure. They have thus achieved a situation in which the people who live in the town feel it as their own, and they are proud of their squares, their church, their ravine and their landscapes.

Yet they also seem to be satisfied with the construction of a golf course, a public initiative, which was opened in 2003, enabling a country town with an ailing economy, thanks to its gradual abandonment of agricultural activity, to bring in new income based on tourism. In addition to this, a five-star, golf-oriented hotel is soon to be opened, this meaning that local residents will be employed in newly created jobs. In response to the criticism that often accompanies such ventures, it might be said that the project is playing a significant regenerative role in the northern zone of Tenerife.

The urban fabric of Buenavista is abruptly interrupted by the ravine known as the Barranco de Triana. This geographical accident, which historically constituted the town's northern limit, cut off the Triana neighbourhood from the old centre. In the 1980s, the town council carried out a project of landscape restoration in and around the ravine, which involved cleaning up around its edges and creating a rural park. In 1995, the "Tenerife Verde" (Green Tenerife) initiative, after analysing the general lack of green spaces in the island, proposed a series of initiatives in order to furnish Tenerife with facilities of an appropriate level. The activities were divided into eleven lots, with Buenavista coming under the heading of number nine. The project breathed new life into the town's urban fabric by creating a network of walkers' routes connecting access to the ravine parklands and the municipal nerve centre, the Remedios Church, with three other strategic points that have also been refurbished. One, situated on the far side of the ravine, is the Plaza de Triana, while the other two, the Plaza del Chorro and the Parque de San Francisco, are in the old town centre. In the latter case, the ruins of the old San Francisco Convent have been protected from the visual impact of some adjacent sporting facilities by means of a series of tree-planted banks. In the access area to the park there is a new drinks stand that has become a popular meeting point.

The completion of this series of small-scale surgical operations is along the lines of a strategy that is in keeping with the urban scale. While the points of action are specifically targeted, the procedure guarantees that the limited public investment involved has a ripple effect on the urban structure of Buenavista, where the old town centre and the Triana neighbourhood are definitively reunited.

PROJECT **Green Tenerife [Site 9], Buenavista del Norte, Canary Islands, Spain**
DATE **2002**
AUTHORS **GPY Arquitectos: Juan Antonio González Pérez, Urbano Yanes Tuña, Félix Perera Pérez**
DEVELOPER **Tenerife Insular Council, Buenavista del Norte City Council**
SURFACE **8,793.15 m²**
COST **414,457.55 €**

Interventions: 1. Plaza de los Remedios (existent) / 2. San Francisco Park / 3. Plaza de Triana / 4. Plaza del Chorro / 5. Pedestrian System / 6. Barranco de Triana (urban park)

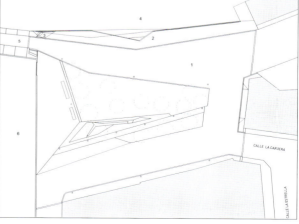

Plaza de Triana plan: 1. Dual-use pedestrian zone / 2. Look-out point / 3. Public drinking fountain / 4. Barranco de Triana (ravine) / 5. Access to the ravine / 6. Schoolyard

Accordingly, the urban structure now established in the town has recently been joined by a new tourist-related element: a seaside walk around the edge of the golf course with spectacular views and recently installed municipal facilities. It is a new attraction for the town whose inhabitants are now seeing how increasing numbers of tourists are making the most of their stay, coming to visit the town, to have a coffee in the Plaza de la Remedios thus fostering the 'power to mingle groups', to take photos of the old convent and hike in the ravine that links up with the footpath around the golf course – and who knows whether this might be a stimulus to reopening the San Francisco drinks stand so that people can enjoy a beer in the park.

It remains, perhaps, to reflect on the new breed of tourist who visits the town, a tourist who comes to see the centre of Buenavista, who is curious about the place and, rather than staying confined to the hotel, prefers to enjoy the island. This tourist seeks the traditional and typical features of the place, while also discovering that there exists another kind of architecture that does not erase the earlier style or imitate it either, an architecture that is searching for connections and relationships and that coexists with other elements. In this regard, we are probably moving forward, as citizens and as tourists. There is no doubt that Buenavista is already showing the way.

Marina Romero, architect based in Las Palmas de Gran Canaria and former director of BASA magazine.

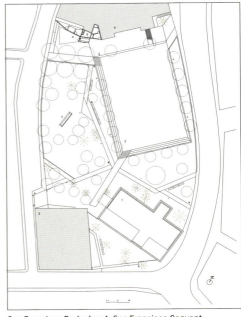

San Francisco Park plan: 1. San Francisco Convent (ruin) / 2. Sports field / 3. Civil Guard living quarters / 4. Municipal offices / 5. Drinks kiosk / 6. Covered terrace / 7. Public drinking fountain

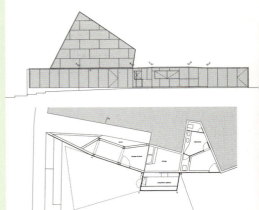

Kiosk: Unfolded skin and Plan

2002

Zuera

Regeneration of the River Gállego and Environs

ALDAYJOVER ARQUITECTURA Y PAISAJE

[JOINT WINNER]
2002

Bullrings[1] in the River
LUIS FRANCISCO ESPLÁ

I am obsessed by balance. Since I was very young, eight years old and a novice at judo, I have understood that existence is a delicate game of stability. Later, my close ties with the countryside, animals and nature enlarged this sense, showing me the extent to which it is necessary to achieve concord between beings and their setting, so as to bring into being the harmony that guarantees survival.

This balance can never be static as it is a purely aesthetic aspiration. Contemplation is the desire to be excluded from the organic cosmos, which has an integrating and, above all, dynamic disposition, so that one might pursue, unencumbered, the metaphysical.

The simple fact of walking and, by extension, living, is nothing but a succession of imbalances necessarily provoked and always compensated for by their corresponding stabilising reactions. This is, in essence, existence, and the principle can be applied to human nature at every level, whether it is organic, intellectual or social.

From the intellectual standpoint one divines what some call spirit, others soul, or simply consciousness. This is a subtle sieve through which the sensorial world loses its objective condition to become a personal reality. It is here, then, that the alchemy of creation happens.

The capacity to *aestheticise* is born in the individual, already tinged with his or her own features. The subjective aspect of artistic production and its need to be detached from practical reality shuns any content that is not purely that of artistic logic. In brief, the aesthetic criterion is a born upsetter of balance. This is why it is difficult to believe that, making the most of the slight concavity of a bend in the River Gállego – and as if calling on it to disregard the comings and goings of its course – the bullrings of Zuera could have been placed there without spoiling this once-endangered setting.

If I have started out by speaking of balance it is because, with this intervention – where the tremendous

1. *The original title 'Arenas en el río' has a double meaning, impossible to capture simultaneously in English. 'Arena' can mean sand or grit, or bullring (arena). Hence, apart from its decidedly poetic ring, it refers to a before and an after, to the before of the sands and grit that silted up the river, endangering the town and its environs, and the after of the public facility of the arena that was installed as part of the project [translator].*

allegorical charge of its elements would guarantee serious conflict in advance – the voice of Solomon calls into being the harmony of a perfect braid: architecture, symbolism and nature.

Perhaps the success of this communion lies in the sagacious modesty with which the project is administered: in the desire not to build – in this case – physically on the land; in making us believe that the space occupied by the arena was always there, as yet another gift from its fluvial generosity; and that the promontory that accommodates the tiers of seating rose up all by itself so as to cover up the hullabaloo of the festivals. Nevertheless, anyone who is able to read beyond what is material will see – no, rather *feel* – the intimacy of its harmonies. On the one hand is the river as an evocation of time: the dynamic, that which flows and passes, what is gone, evidence of beginning and end, imperfection, the uncontainable, predetermination, destiny, what is extinguished, life in itself. On the other, the constant circle and profile of the bullrings harbour the contrary: the esoteric, the immovable, the inextinguishable, the fadeless, perfection and the eternal, the unreachable, the divinity.

In the midst of all this, as if it were not enough, are all the readings summoned up by bullfighting. I shall only distil from these the main argument, in the words of Miquel Barceló: «Bulls belong to the mechanisms that man has devised against death». Evidently these also include religion, art and the most infallible of all, love. All of them are tricks whereby we fashion the fiction of our supremacy in the face of death, short-lived balsam against the certainty of our destiny. To sum up, they are brief fits of immortality, as innocent as they are useless.

Yet without the substance of these lies, existence would be unbearable.

Thanks to the work of Margarita Jover and Iñaki Alday, dialogue between these two worlds, the magic and the real, is propitiated. The circle of the curiosity of the waters is opened up so that they, in turn, irrigate at the zenith of their flooding the mysteries of the concentric. And after recreating their flow in the setting where death is conjured up and banished, they have the good fortune of delaying their course, of prolonging their luck. They will return to their bed, their course. They will return just as the spectator returns to everyday tasks after the bullfight, but this time they are transported by the heady, redemptive sense of the imperishable.

Luis Francisco Esplá, artist and bullfighter.

For decades, the relationship between Zuera and the River Gállego was hostile. The continual dumping of rubbish and progressive accumulation of gravel thanks to frequent flooding considerably reduced the hydraulic capacity of the river basin. This caused a rise in the average water level, the disappearance of a number of islands and compounded the erosive effects on the town-side bank. With its array of municipal equipment, residences, farms and workshops, this bank had been developed facing away from the river. The possibility of definitive reconciliation, a long yearned-for goal of a series of post-Franco municipal governments, came with the turn of the century. The Confederación Hidrográfica del Ebro (River Ebro Hydrographical Confederation), which is responsible for managing the river basin, provided the necessary funds for work on an intervention that would manage such disparate elements as the increased

Normal flow

High water flow

Rising waters

hydraulic capacity of the river basin, protection against erosion, preservation of the natural corridor, improving water quality, planning and orienting the urban front towards the river, and creating a civic space that would be able to accommodate collective uses. The project dealt with the difference of levels separating town and river by breaking it into three interconnected terraces that would flood progressively and in an orderly fashion when the waters rose. The concavity of one of the terraces has provided a space for an amphitheatre which is the venue for meetings, concerts, sporting events and Zuera's traditional, annually-held bull festival. A footbridge gives pedestrian access to an island which has been created as a natural reserve with an observatory. The intervention has destined a good part of its budget to infrastructural operations that are essential but barely visible, thereby resolving the problematic confrontation between town and river, while also conquering a public space loaded with civic connotations, which unfolds by means of austere, subtle urban planning that faces out in the transition from one element to the other.

PROJECT **Regeneration of the River Gállego and Environs, Zuera, Spain**
DATE **2001**
AUTHORS **aldajover arquitectura y paisaje, Iñaki Alday, Margarita Jover, María Pilar Sancho**
DEVELOPER **Zuera City Council, Confederación Hidrográfica del Ebro**
SURFACE **168,000 m²**
COST **2,288,240 €**

Bullring

Leipzig
Lene Voigt Park
BÜRO KIEFER

[JOINT WINNER]
2002

Between Industrial Past and Postindustrial Present

ARNOLD BARTETZKY

A sad state of affairs. Some of the hopes that drove the planning of Lene Voigt place over a decade ago have gone unfulfilled. The plot of land once occupied by Eilenburg railway station has not yet become the 'flourishing landscape' promised by the originators of the project and the city – a place that would manifest the sense of community and the vitality of the neighbourhood.

A stroll through the current site presents one or the other experience of disillusionment. The paths are strewn with rubbish, and a walk across the meadow at the heart of the 1km x 100m strip of park resembles a slalom between piles of dog mess. The sculptural elements have been covered with graffiti, the majority of the park benches have been devastated. Even the low wall made of supposedly indestructible gabions – blocks of bricks and wood beam held together with rebar – that divide the grass from the garden plots running along the main axis of the park have fallen victim to vandalism. If one gazes beyond the birch-lined wall, empty lots yawn back. The garden plots offered to the local residents for their own use haven't been met with any interest. That is all the more disappointing, since the provision of semi-private plots was originally seen as one of the most convincing elements of the plan for the park. The idea was to awaken the slumbering creative potential in a working-class neighbourhood plagued by unemployment. The emptiness of the garden plots conveys the reaction of the community to the invitation to join in the development of the park: no interest.

In the face of the neglect and partial decay of the park, designed by the Berlin-based Büro Kiefer and completed in 2003, one wonders where all the active citizens involved in the planning have gone. After all, the involvement of the locals' ideas through public workshops was considered an especially progressive feature of the project. Apparently, the one-time activists failed to overcome the inertia and indifference of the majority of the population – and particularly the appetite for destruction on the part of a socially precarious minority.

Even if in hindsight the vision of making a sustainable contribution to activating the citizens and encouraging them to identify with their neighbourhood was an all too idealistic assumption, it wasn't a poor decision to award Lene Voigt Park the European Prize for Urban Public Space. Not just because the vision was worth the test of reality, but above all because, in spite of its deficits, the park has significantly improved the quality of life in Reudnitz. There could hardly have been a wiser use for the site of the old train station, lying fallow since the 1940s, than to transform it into a green lung for this densely built neighbourhood near the city centre.

The intervention, however, did not follow a tabula rasa approach; rather, the intention was to build a bridge between an industrial past and a postindustrial present by integrating architectural relics from the 19th and 20th centuries. Not only were the old trees preserved, but also the remains of the train station, an engine shed, railroader dwellings and fragments of the surrounding walls. Even an above-ground heating pipe has been integrated into the park design.

The park runs along a main axis outlined by a large grass area and a wide path. The unobtrusive design elements, such as rows of stele-like steel plates, mark the borders between the functional areas and accentuate the lines of the neighbouring streets tied into the park's own system of pathways. Unlike the garden plots on the northern side of the park, the south side with its playgrounds and sports fields surrounded by robinias and hedges cater to the real needs of the locals, who have in fact taken advantage of them.

The park has also had a plainly positive effect on the state of the neighbourhood architecture, dominated by the high-quality houses of the late 19th and early 20th centuries, but suffering under low occupancy and decay. Now, made more attractive by the view of the park, most of the adjacent apartment buildings have been refurbished. But Reudnitz district is not the park's sole beneficiary. Linking up with a path for cycling and walking that continues on into a former, tree-lined railway path, the park is part of a long greenbelt offering an environmentally friendly connection between Leipzig's city centre and the eastern boroughs.

It remains uncertain whether the locals will someday make Lene Voigt Park their own to the degree hoped for by the planners. That would require more meticulous care on the part of the city. And in the long run, that will depend in turn on the development of a civic sense of neighbourhood responsibility, which until now has been particularly lacking in the cities of postcommunist Europe.

Arnold Bartetzky, researcher at the Centre for the History and Culture of East Central Europe in Leipzig.

At the end of the 20th century, the Leipzig neighbourhood of Reudnitz was having to deal with structural problems such as lack of free space, a lot of unoccupied housing and the uncomfortable presence of a closed site of over 6 hectares that broke up the urban fabric: the abandoned land of Eilenburg Station, which had been destroyed in Allied bombing attacks during the Second World War. All that remained of the former infrastructure were some clusters of railway lines, a few subsidiary buildings, a train shed and a very large heating pipe. After years of mobilising, the residents and the council initiated a participative process in order to turn the land into a public park. Going beyond the merely propositional phase of the project, the citizens' participation

also involved them in some of the construction work and subsequent park management. Some of the pre-existing industrial elements that defined the idiosyncrasy of the place were preserved, for example, the train shed and the monumental heating pipe. The site, in the shape of a long strip organised around an axial footpath with a series of transversal paths giving continuity to adjacent streets, is subdivided into three longitudinal sections. The central part is clear, consisting of a sequence of grassy patches that replace the former rail space of the station, while the two perimeter strips are more densely packed, combining a series of small plots with specific functions. Those on the southern border contain children's playing areas, petanque spaces, ping-pong tables and sandy areas for beach volleyball. On the northern side are garden plots rented out to the residents along with compact container-sheds in a variety of colours for storing the gardening tools.

The alien body that once obstructed and tore apart the urban fabric is now a connecting agent giving continuity to the streets of Reudnitz. Without renouncing the memory of its industrial past, the intervention has turned the land into a civic meeting place, which is particularly close to the citizens who have conceived it, constructed it and taken possession of it.

PROJECT **Lene Voigt Park (former Stadtteilpark Reudnitz Park), Leipzig, Germany**
DATE **1998-2003**
AUTHORS **Büro Kiefer, Landschaftarchitektur, Gabriele G. Kiefer**
DEVELOPER **Stadt Leipzig Grünflächenamt & Amt für Stadtsanierung und Wohnbauförderung**
SURFACE **60,000 m²**
COST **5,120,000 €**

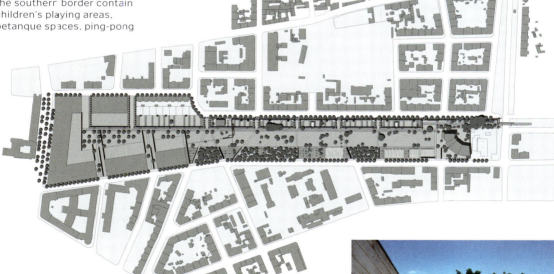

General plan

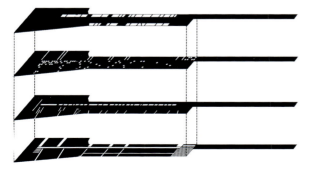

Showing uses

Targeted Intervention

HANS IBELINGS

For ten years now, Westblaak Skatepark has been a popular and much-used public space in the centre of Rotterdam. The intensive use underscores the success of this intervention which can be seen as an assembly of elements designed by several different parties at the request of Rotterdam Development Corporation (OBR). The overall design of the Skatepark was by Dirk van Peijpe of the Rotterdam Urban Planning and Public Housing Agency (dS+V), while the colourful pattern of the surfacing was devised by graphic design studio 75B. The stainless-steel skate equipment (driveways, a pyramid with curb, a spine, various quarters, banks, kerb, a mini ramp with two extensions and a wide vert ramp) were designed and produced by Solos International. There is a container-like kiosk for the management of the type that architect Joost Glissenaar designed as a standard storage shed for Rotterdam playgrounds, and there is a café designed by Jeroen Hoorn. With its gabion facades filled with stone and glass, this little building is an unmistakable tribute to Herzog & de Meuron's 1998 Dominus Winery in California.

Before the arrival of the Skatepark, this location was little more than a glorified median strip. Apart from the occasional individual who spent part of his or her lunch break here, it was an overlooked area, one of the countless underused spaces in the centre of Rotterdam, a city that suffers, even more than many other cities, from an excess of public space. The city centre is a textbook example of modernist open urban planning, with free-standing buildings marooned in a sea of space, so that there are just too few people and activities to fill all the empty spaces. For that reason alone, this dedicated programming of a public space has been a definite improvement.

Considering how intensively it is used, one decade on the Skatepark is looking good, and well maintained. Like many parks, the Skatepark has its own set of rules. But the long list of dos and don'ts in force here should not be interpreted as evidence of government control of public space. In this case it is completely logical, given the increased risk of collisions, broken bones and concussion that skate boarding, in-line skating and BMX riding involve. The fact that the park cannot be locked makes it clear enough that this is not a quasi-public but a genuinely public space.

The Skatepark is inherently mono-functional. Without skateboard, in-line skates or BMX bike you don't have much reason to be there. And so you don't go there, which is made easier by the fact that this is an enclave surrounded by traffic. That the café was conceived as a point of contact between skaters and passers-by is all very nice, but overly optimistic for the reality, which is that the Skatepark, including the café, is a world of its own in the city.

That said, the Skatepark's mono-functional programming is perfectly in tune with Rotterdam where, especially during festivals like the summer carnival, street races and the marathon, public space in the city centre is used intensively for a single event. As soon as the event is over, it disappears only to pop up again exactly one year later.

Anyone who takes the view that the essence of the public domain is the encounter with the other, cannot but conclude that this Skatepark does not work. It is patronised exclusively by skaters. On the other hand, they do at least come here, and for years, day in day out, the park has been their place. The fact that it is young people who have appropriated the park is another reason for enthusiasm. There is little space for them in the city centre and almost no part of the built environment where their needs are taken seriously into account. Those too old for the playground, must find their own ways of amusing themselves in the city. And this in defiance of the fact that even in an ageing European society, one quarter of the population is under 20. Places like this Skatepark are very rare, much too rare.

Hans Ibelings, architectural historian and director of A10 new European architecture.

Despite its prominence within the urban fabric of Rotterdam, few pedestrians used to venture on to the central strip of Westblaak Avenue, which was cut off between two lateral roads, each with a large volume of traffic. When considering the need to give this space a specific use that would make it dynamic and attractive, the city council decided to devote it to skateboarders. Accustomed to making intensive use of public space, this group frequently arouses ill-feeling among the public and does not always find suitable places for getting together. After some new zebra crossings were opened up to

upgrade accessibility, the perimeter of the pavement was protected from the traffic by two rows of linden trees and a laurel hedge one and a half metres high. The pre-existing pavement was replaced by a continuous layer of coloured asphalt, making the entire surface suitable for skating. Eleven large metal pieces with concave surfaces, especially designed with the direct involvement of groups of skateboarders, roller-skaters and BMX riders and suitable for use by amateurs and professionals alike, were set into the asphalt. A small free-standing building which closes off one end houses a cafeteria, a number of public facilities and a maintenance shed.

The central strip of Westblaak is now a much sought-after space both by people who engage in different kinds of sports on wheels and visitors who, attracted by their spectacular acrobatics, are curious enough to cross the busy perimeter roads. The judicious solution here gratifies the skateboarders who now have their own space in which to meet, others who did not look kindly on their spreading through the city's public spaces; and, finally, the city as a whole, which has regained the collective sense of a space that was once without uses or attributes.

PROJECT **Skatepark in Westblaak Avenue, Rotterdam, Netherlands**
DATE **2001**
AUTHORS **dS+V Rotterdam, Dirk van Peijpe**
PARTICIPANTS **Studio 75B**
DEVELOPER **City of Rotterdam**
SURFACE **6,700 m²**
COST **1,179,829 €**

Espinho
Programme of Urban Rehabilitation in Marinha de Silvade District
SÁRRIA–JÚNIOR

[SPECIAL MENTION]
2002

Along the Seafront
ANA VAZ MILHEIRO

The amazing proliferation of [urban waterfront] projects, from modest and simple to more ambitious and complex versions, has enabled the reestablishment of the symbolic importance of interaction between urban constructions and a proximity to water in this end-of-century period. At the same time, the results show the degree of success in replacing previous economic activities, which produced excessive environmental and production costs.
Nuno Portas, On the Recent Transformations in Waterfronts, 1999

During the 1990s, Portugal increased public investment in waterfronts and riverside areas, replicating the model of the 1998 Lisbon World Exhibition, a revitalisation process which started in 1993, causing heated public debate. On quite different scales, Portuguese cities discovered strong urban development potential in their waterfronts, as is suggested by Nuno Portas in the epigraph. This was true not only on the speculative plane, earmarking these areas for housing and highly specialised commercial purposes, but also by rezoning obsolete industrial areas. These industries – often connected to declining economic activities like fishing or non-competitive industries such as textiles – had seen their perimeters encroached on by a progressively impoverished and socially marginalised population.
The Municipality of Espinho consists of a county with a population of 33,701 inhabitants. The town, of an average size in the national context, is located on the coast of northern Portugal. Following this discussion, Espinho began to consider some of its residential areas which had presented problems of social and economic sustainability, as was the case of Bairro da Marinha, in the parish of Silvade. In addition, the city became aware of its strong tourist vocation, bolstered by a considerable stretch of beach and served by a major rail infrastructure, the Lisbon-Porto line.
The area of Bairro da Marinha, located in an area of high landscape integration, along the seafront, posed an interesting challenge, and it seemed like a case that could become exemplary in this type of intervention. Its historically relevant yet now defunct industrial character made it eligible for a multidisci-

plinary urban planning operation, which would not only cover the 'design', but also include an action plan focused on combating social segregation, illiteracy, poverty and unemployment.

Within this integrated vision, the Bairro da Marinha de Silvade Urban Rehabilitation Programme (PRUM) was launched in 1997. Architects Carlos A. Sárria and João Paulo Júnior led the team developing the proposed reclassification. The intervention focused on rehabilitating the Bairro Novo (New Neighbourhood), a residential structure consisting of seven blocks of city council-promoted housing dating from 1965, two school facilities and a century-old canning factory. The landscape plan also included recovery of the bed and banks of the Ribeira de Silvalde, a waterline previously used as a dumping ground, over a 400-metre extension between the railroad tracks and the sea. This became the neighbourhood's image, transforming what was formerly seen as a barrier to urban continuity into a point of attraction. The strategy rested on a very precise performance, identifying problems and acting on a small scale in order to transfer and consolidate all the surroundings. By demolishing illegal structures and repairing existing, seriously rundown buildings, by paving public spaces and creating leisure areas that would be readily identifiable by local people — such as the new squares — different occupational dynamics were generated. During the intervention, methods of community involvement were tested, such as environmental education and multi-cultural activities, aimed at different age groups.

Criteria for durability and ease of maintenance guided the choices made, namely for the materials palette. Support for the fishing activities still practised was reflected in the realignment of the existing pier and the creation of specific fishing areas.

This project in Espinho, completed in 2002, shows the maturity of thought that has characterised Portuguese architects on the issue of waterfront interventions, enhanced by interaction with international debates. Working with the local population and with a focus on micro intervention, this was an experience that accrued to the community, strengthening architecture's vocation as a public service, which has unfortunately not always been upheld.

Ana Vaz Milheiro, Lisbon-based architecture critic.

The fishing neighbourhood of Marinha de Silvade was once cut off from the rest of the urban fabric of Espinho by the railway line, as well as being confined between the barriers constituted by the waterfront, an extensive private property and an abandoned canning factory. In the 1980s, the closing down of the industry, a major source of employment, aggravated the precarious situation of an urban sector that was afflicted by the scourges of unemployment, social exclusion and illiteracy. Moreover, the River Silvade, a polluted watercourse that was used as a rubbish tip, split the neighbourhood into two badly-connected parts.
In 1996, and with a view to eliminating these physical and social barriers, the council approved a programme of urban rehabilitation consisting of 22 specific interventions in single plan of phased implementation. Seven blocks of state-subsidised housing were reformed, along with two schools and the 20th-century factory-workers' houses, while the factory itself was refurbished and turned into a cultural centre. A new nursery school was constructed as well as a residence for the elderly. Again, two new buildings were constructed with 50 state-subsidised dwellings and the public space was consolidated with renovated paving, garden areas and street furniture as well as an underground refuse collection system. The environmental recuperation and improved landscaping of the Silvade shoreline was accompanied by the construction of new bridges and the creation of a river park. The refurbishment of the seafront included the renovation of beaches and of a breakwater where facilities were installed in a special space for fishing.

The result constitutes irrefutable proof that transversal, holistic planning based on improving urban space, enhancing public facilities, rehabilitating heritage buildings and spaces and recovering natural resources can have very significant effects in improving a city's social and physical reality.

PROJECT **Programme of Urban Rehabilitation in Marinha de Silvade District, Espinho, Portugal**
DATE **2002**
AUTHORS **Carlos A. Sárria, João Paulo Júnior**
PARTICIPANT **Carlos Alberto Silva**
DEVELOPER **Cámara Municipal de Espinho**
SURFACE **195,000 m²**
COST **2,271,171 €**

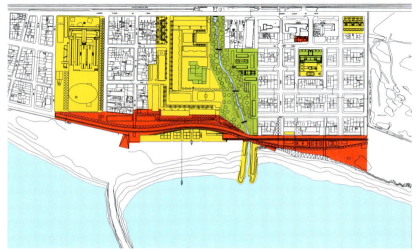

General plan

Barcelona, Montcada i Reixac, Santa Coloma de Gramenet, Sant Adrià de Besòs

Environmental Regeneration of the River Besòs

BARCELONA REGIONAL

[SPECIAL MENTION]
2002

From Limit to Generative Centre

ORIOL BOHIGAS

Traditionally, and with different intentions and in terms bordering on the symbolic, we consider that the geographical setting of the city of Barcelona is the plain running from the Collserola range to the sea and from river to river. The two rivers are the Llobregat and the Besòs. Yet this condition of boundaries we have assigned to them does not exactly coincide with the reality. The successive growth spurts of the city now oblige us to see them not as limits but as central axes of new urban areas pointing in two directions, one southwest and the other northeast, marking the genesis of the most immediate metropolitan area. This reality is particularly evident and also frequently conflictive along the northeast line, which is to say the surroundings of the River Besòs.

The Besòs today is a torrential river subject to sudden great variations of flow: it seems that it can go from the extremes of 5 metres of water per second to 1,000 metres. The basic bed attributed to it has an average width of some 150 metres and is almost 10 kilometres long in the reach that affects the urban area of several municipalities (Barcelona, Montcada i Reixac, Santa Coloma de Gramenet, Sant Adrià de Besòs). In other words, this is a surface area of approximately 150 hectares, a very considerable space in both qualitative and quantitative terms in the central part of the metropolitan area. It was therefore evident that the whole sector needed reorganisation and this is the aim of the public space project under discussion here.

The environmental refurbishment of the Besòs bed, which has now been successfully and fruitfully achieved, presented three overlapping issues: the hydraulic regulation of a torrential stream, the periodical heavy flooding of which has caused major catastrophes; making the most of the spaces spreading out from the watercourse for collective leisure activities; and creating a representative axis that would generate an urban order along the facades of the municipalities and neighbourhoods it runs through. In other words, what was required was a river park subject to all these conditions despite the difficulties involved since they were frequently not complementary but contradictory and even, at times, incompatible. It should be recognised, however, that this large number of almost autonomous claims has been used as a basis of the project's creative genesis. Perhaps its essential quality is precisely the use of the basic indispensable elements required for resolving each issue as secondary but also indispensable elements in all the others. An intelligent search for coincidences is the creative framework.

One primordial factor in the gradual channelling of the watercourse has been the construction of a riverbed on two levels: a lower central line that holds the permanent, smaller flows and a higher extension that accommodates the big floods. This is used to create, at the upper level, areas that are normally not flooded and that can be used as leisure spaces most of the year. In these zones, vegetation that resists the predictable periodical flooding is planted, so that the dual function of the space raises in itself the basic argument of its gardening scheme.

The water flowing in the lower channel has to be regulated by means of transversal barriers, which is to say automatically inflating and deflating dams. This mechanism creates surfaces of still water at different levels that blend into the landscape of the leisure areas in visual relationship with both sides of the course of the river.

The ramps of access and emergency exit for the second-level areas, which have to go up to the normal levels of the urban surrounds are expressively and forcefully integrated into the continuous line of the large retaining wall. This structure could be anodyne and amorphous but the ramps are used to 'architecturise' and 'urbanise' an element whose origins are simply to be found in the need for hydraulic regularisation so that it has now become an explicit foundation of a range of urban occurrences.

We might keep analysing other elements of this intelligent project, all of them coinciding with the desire to use a matter of hydraulic engineering as an urban planning theme in a zone with many environmental problems. Hence Barcelona and its Metropolitan Area have acquired a new 150-hectare park, a small sample of the great northeast park that Cerdà once drew up, with an excess of generosity and perhaps utopia, in his Eixample Plan.

Oriol Bohigas, Barcelona-based architect and urban planner.

General plan

With a basin populated by more than two million inhabitants, the River Besòs has been profoundly changed by human action, especially its lower reaches which are markedly industrial and urban. True to the pattern of the Mediterranean river, its average volume is greatly reduced although it is also periodically subject to sudden flooding. In 1962, after a catastrophic flood, the last 9-kilometre section running into the mouth was channelled between two 4-metre-high retaining walls, which delimit a bed 130 metres wide. The agreement signed in 1995 between the four municipalities lining the river – Barcelona, Santa Coloma de Gramenet, Sant Adrià de Besòs and Montcada i Reixac – sought to minimise the dismembering impact of this public works initiative in the urban zones that had turned their backs on the river.

In the upper section of this reach, the bed is presently meandriform, which slows the flow of the water and increases the river's biodiversity. Ten hectares of inaccessible marshlands on both sides of the river function as a natural water-purifying plant. However, in the lower section, there are 13 hectares of fields open to the public by way of ramps set into the protecting walls and leading up to a new riverside walk located on the urban side. In this part of the river, the channel has been widened by 20 to 50 metres and five inflatable dams have been installed, these generating lagoons that function as independent water purifiers and deflate automatically when the river floods. Thanks to the complex cooperation between several branches of the administration at different levels, the bed of the River Besòs has now ceased to be a marginal barrier to become an integrating element that stitches the urban fabric back together. The application of pioneering hydraulic solutions has made it possible to turn this zone into a biologically rich river park that is also a sustainable, environmentally-friendly water-purifying plant, while also inviting citizens to enjoy a civic space on the metropolitan scale.

PROJECT **Environmental Regeneration of the River Besòs, Barcelona, Montcada i Reixac, Santa Coloma de Gramenet, Sant Adrià de Besòs, Spain**
DATE **2000**
AUTHORS **Barcelona Regional, Antoni Alarcón, Ferran Puig, Bernardo de Sola**
DEVELOPER **Barcelona City Council, Montcada i Reixac City Council, Santa Coloma de Gramenet City Council, Mancomunitat de Municipis [AMB], Consorci per a la Defensa del Riu Besòs**
SURFACE **804,806 m²**
COST **19,983,652 €**

2000

Mollet del Vallès

Can Mulà

SERRA-VIVES-CARTAGENA ARQUITECTES

[JOINT WINNER]
2000

From Suburbia to Centrality
MONTSERRAT TURA

I remember, as if it were right now, when I received, at the Centre of Contemporary Culture of Barcelona, the first of the prizes – ten years ago now – awarded by this institution in recognition of the creativeness put into urban transformation initiatives in which treatment of public space was the foremost concern.

As if it were right now, I relive with emotion the meaning of that prize for a town like Mollet del Vallès where, after the 1960s, the large influx of immigrants from that inequitable Spain of the Franco regime arrived and found less than 10,000 inhabitants, all of them engaged in agriculture or, frequently, working in the textile and leather industries.

The neighbourhoods, devoid of services, spread in an uncoordinated fashion without any prior urban scheme. They consisted of scattered blocks of buildings wherever property developers had acquired a bit of agricultural land at a good price. The huge task of our – fortunately recuperated – democratic government ensured that public works were not only a way of creating jobs in times of crisis but also a major element of social cohesion. Great avenues and erstwhile malodorous streams, now boulevards, were structuring a city where none had existed.

In the mid-20h century, true cities were being built in many parts of Europe while, in Barcelona and its metropolitan area, construction continued to be chaotic. The Can Mulà Special Plan made the most of a hole that had been left by the devastating textile industry crisis of the 1970s. The old factory premises threatened to end up as rubble after two decades of neglect and the council put a new burst of energy into acquiring this space, which had become central thanks to the spread of the working-class neighbourhoods in the 1960s.

The idea then – and this is what we did – was to enlarge the centre. This small historic heart of a county town that now had over 50,000 inhabitants grew in keeping with new urban development legislation in which, proportionally, the area assigned for public space and facilities was especially significant and of very high quality in architectural terms.

The new council building, the municipal market, the multiplex cinema, the large area of public space converted into a shopping boulevard and the parks surrounding the whole project conferred a quality of urban landscape beyond our wildest dreams. The first escalators in stainless steel and glass as materials of public urban infrastructure, the marble and fine hardwood were all made available to the people of the town who had once been obliged to think that good taste and quality architecture were reserved for the powerful.

Over this decade, the citizens have literally taken over the streets of Mollet and crowds of people out for a stroll fill the footpaths and squares, while children and their parents play on luxuriant grass stretching out like a great lawn rug. Teenagers have fallen in love here and music has resounded…

The market is still one of the best there is and it has enticed people of all ages. With effort, the public space has been conserved with the quality that so dazzled us at the time.

The multiplex cinema has been closed by short-sighted private enterprise unable to see beyond the cashbox and, in keeping with the laws of the wretched domino effect, some high-quality business premises have also closed. Their substitution by other types of trade is a trend that should be avoided and the re-opening of the cinemas (with renewed effort from the local administration) has become necessary so that what was the main project of urban renovation does not show signs of fatigue.

Democratic political power cannot lower its guard. Not now. Not ever.

Montserrat Tura, Mollet Mayor (1987-2003).

In the 1970s, the demolition of the Can Mulà textile factory opened up a large open space in the old centre of Mollet, this holding out an unusual opportunity for rethinking the centre of an already-consolidated city. For years, however, the space was only used for the weekly open-air market. It was only after three decades had elapsed that the Mollet Council put up a multi-functional complex consisting of housing, office space, business premises, car parks, a covered municipal market and the new council building. This diversity of uses is consonant with the aim of having a large area of open public space that is permeable to the rest of the town. The new market, its large curved roof giving it representative status, closes off the complex on the north-eastern side. On the north-western edge there is a linear 12-storey housing block of 100 metres in length. The new council building defines the south-western limit of the complex, while the south-eastern boundary is marked by four nine-storey residential blocks separated by interstitial spaces that link the remainder of the old centre with the central space of the new complex. This open area is conceived as consisting of a miscellany of nine small-scale structures built on the large slab covering an underground shopping centre. These free-standing, cubic, two-storey constructions used as business premises both attenuate the impact of the surrounding buildings and break up the public space, giving it a scale that is appropriate to pedestrians.

The result is a magical intersection between two urban scales. The dimensions of the perimeter buildings bring the complex into harmony with the rest of the city, giving it the proper measure of prominence, while the maze of inner spaces confers on the central area a human scale in the style of the typical old quarter of the Mediterranean city. Density, cohesion and formal and functional complexity enhance this Mediterranean character.

PROJECT **Can Mulà, Mollet del Vallès, Spain**
DATE **2000**
AUTHORS **Serra-Vives-Cartagena Arquitectes**
PARTICIPANTS **JSS Associats, Joan Ramon Blasco**
DEVELOPER **Mollet del Vallès City Council, Promosol SA**
SURFACE **12,466 m²**
COST **1,833,086 €**

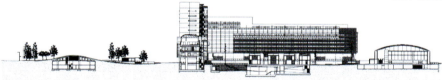

General elevation and plan

Dublin

Smithfield Public Space

MCGARRY NÍ ÉANAIGH ARCHITECTS

[JOINT WINNER]
2000

Old Space, New City
SHANE O'TOOLE

The gas braziers – the highest in the world – have not been lit in a long, long time but Smithfield still smells of horses, thank God. Catching their warm tang transports me back in time, returning for a few indulgent moments to a lost city. Dublin then was a place of musky smells, of animals and men, of tanneries and abattoirs, of sweat and Brylcreem and dark, smoky pubs with bad toilets. Some days the whole city smelled of hops from Guinness's. In summer the Liffey stank to high heaven and on winter nights the sweet scent of turf smoke mingled with the acrid reek of brown coal fires. It's all gone now, along with the sound of milk bottles clinking on doorsteps at dawn, the squeals of animals on their way to slaughter and the echoing street calls of newspaper sellers.

My city has taken on a different ambience. The masculine town of my youth has been sanitized and feminized. Dublin is no longer a rough place of production, but a comfortable centre of consumption. That is why Smithfield is so important to the city and the threat that hangs over it so grave. Smithfield – a rough-textured, cobbled field that takes its fantastic scale from the distillery chimney and 12 giant lighting masts – belongs to 'old' Dublin. And in the eyes of today's city authorities, that is a problem. The vision that led Smithfield's redevelopment as 'the major civic space for Dublin for the 21st century' a decade ago has been lost.

Perhaps the vision was flawed from the outset. The failure to provide underground car parking beneath Smithfield's 300,000 pink, orange, grey, black and blue cobbles was a missed opportunity. Not only would it have provided a long-term source of income for management and maintenance, but it would have added pedestrian animation. Instead, the greatest public space in the city often feels empty and underused.

It all seemed so different when U2 received the Freedom of Dublin and played a concert to launch Smithfield Civic Plaza on March 18th, 2000. The muscular pull of the gritty heart of the city was powerfully felt that cold spring night. Dubliners discovered a new outdoor living room. But the space never really had a chance to develop and bed into the social life of the city. No sooner had Smithfield reopened than its connection to the river and the more affluent south side of town was closed again and turned into a building site. Construction of the *Luas* light rail line at the foot of Smithfield began in 2001 but trams did not run until late 2004.

The derelict west side of Smithfield was redeveloped by 2005 to provide mostly offices and apartments. Tragically, neither of the urban design guidelines proposed by McGarry Ní Éanaigh was enforced by the city authorities. The *genius loci* demanded that the west wall of Smithfield should be of red brick, no more than five storeys high and as plain as possible. Instead, the city got an over-scaled travesty with a façade so busy that the lighting masts almost disappear when seen against it.

A series of eight concerts, featuring acts that included The Buena Vista Social Club and Sting, was planned for 2001, but cancelled early on after local residents grew alienated over lack of consultation and ticketing arrangements. Rows continue to surround the monthly horse fair, made famous in the opening sequence of Alan Parker's film, *The Commitments*. It seems inevitable that sooner or later the city will use health and safety legislation to close it down.

These conflicts have given rise to an 'enhancement plan', partly funded by the European Commission, to 'green and soften' both ends of Smithfield and introduce play equipment for local children this year. But whose space is it, anyway? Does Smithfield belong to the city or just to the few lucky householders whose homes front onto it? Whatever, the city authorities have clearly fallen out of love with Smithfield. Shockingly, the city architect recently called the braziers 'relics' that would never be re-lit. The pagan, flickering flames, with their timeless, mythic quality that so warmed the cockles of this heart, are unlikely to be seen again anytime soon. Smithfield may still smell of horses, but for how much longer, one wonders?

Shane O'Toole, Dublin-based architecture critic and member of the International Committee of Architecture Critics.

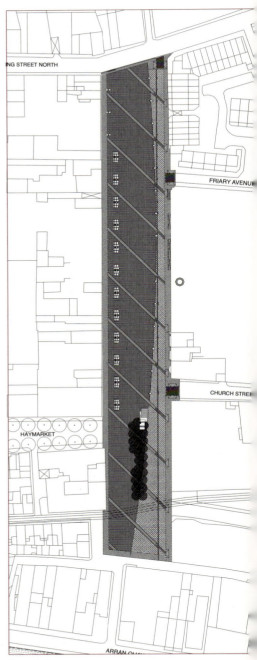

General plan

Centrally located by the River Liffey, Smithfield is a majestic esplanade 335 metres long by 43 metres wide, which was opened in the 17th century for use as a livestock market. The exceptional nature of this empty space within the dense medieval urban fabric of Dublin destined it to be a major focus of social and commercial activity. However, in 1863, when the livestock market was moved elsewhere, the space fell into progressive dereliction, which was aggravated at the end of the 19th century with the closure of a large distillery fronting on to the space. All that remains of it today is a 38-metre-high chimney. In the 20th century, lack of public investment and the indiscriminate presence of private vehicles saw Smithfield's decline into a run-down, residual space. With the recent turn of the century, the Dublin City Council planned a series of projects to improve the historic centre of the city. The renovation of Smithfield, which began in 1997 with the call for ideas in an international competition, became the standard-bearing project of the overall strategy. The intervention began with clearing the esplanade of cars, turning it into an exclusively pedestrian precinct. The clearing operation uncovered the original cobblestone paving which was respected and reinforced. Parallel strips of white granite cross the pavement diagonally, conferring on it a unitary rhythm in keeping with the scale of the esplanade. However, the recuperated empty space also accentuated the heterogeneity of the facades of an array of buildings that were very diverse in terms of their age, type and height. Hence, twelve 27-metre-high lighting masts were installed on the western front, thereby pulling together and emphasising the directionality of the space while also bestowing on it new symbolic and orderly elevation. In its simplicity and forcefulness, the project effectively achieves perceptive unification of the esplanade and gives it the identity it needed in order to become Dublin's foremost civic space.

PROJECT **Smithfield Public Space, Dublin, Ireland**
DATE **1999**
AUTHORS **McGarry Ní Éanaigh Architects**
DEVELOPER **Dublin Corporation - Bardas Átha Cliath**
SURFACE **14,405 m²**
COST **4,400,000 €**

Girona
Central Ter Park

FRANCESC HEREU & JOAQUIM ESPAÑOL

[SPECIAL MENTION]
2000

Listening to the Inaudible
ANTONI PUIGVERD

After passing through a series of swamps, the River Ter is depleted and sluggish by the time it reaches Girona. When the architects were commissioned for this project of creating the park and river in its present form of a pool of placid waters, the landscape was pure devastation. The riverbed had been devastated by a clay extraction plant. On one bank no plants grew, while the other had become a free-for-all rubble tip with a thriving population of rats. The waters were stagnant, fetid and foul. For centuries, this had been an outlying part of the city of Girona, which explains its neglect. However, at the end of the 20th century, the city's expansion required crossing to the other side of the River Ter, thus making this reach of the river quite central. On one side, there is the Devesa forest (of centenarian plane trees and the grounds of the modern fair precinct and auditorium) and, on the other bank, is the virtually new neighbourhood of Fontajau which, coming from the river, begins with the sports pavilion.

The architects Español and Hereu approached this context by listening to the spirit of the place. The first priority was to ensure that nature would take over again, as if it had never been expelled. The once-degraded place is now idyllic. Yet the architects' work is barely visible: it is the expression of a type of architecture we would have to define as 'accommodating' in contrast with the present fashion of 'tyrannical' or exhibitionist architecture. First of all, they transformed the feeble trickle of the river's course into a large pool of calm water where bulrushes grow, ducks swim, fish abound and migratory birds stop over. In order to achieve this, they introduced a small weir, which is hidden by the water itself. The bank where nothing used to grow is now covered in green.

Across the river, the intervention is still less visible: the architects had to introduce a wall to contain the river in case of flooding and to protect the zone where the sports pavilion is built. While the work of the wall is solid and complex, it is hidden beneath a gentle rise of the ground, a green wave that runs in a straight line accentuated by a poplar-lined path and defining the perimeter of an immense, almost empty field. The uncluttered space of the field bestows an exceptional quality on the park. It is exceptional because our architecture tends, even when designing green zones, to express *horror vacui*. Yet this is a large green plain, its flatness only broken by a few apple trees, a great field that, when it meets the river, ends with a discrete fishermen's wharf. It is at this point that we discover the architects' signature, the only expressive detail, in the form of a tilted cement cube at the water's edge, alongside other smaller cubes that constitute a breakwater. Subtly pierced, the cube with its holes evokes in an essentialist way the constructions that once exploited the river's course. It is a sort of chapel that guards the spirit of the place. Someone has added a touch of graffiti and birds nest in it, while the reeds and water lilies reinforce its feeling of strangeness and neglect.

On the side away from the water, the field lines the steps of the sports pavilion which now become tiered seating. From here one can contemplate the cathedral standing out over the high plane trees of the Devesa forest while, in the foreground, the eyes are soothed by the peaceful waters, the green of the field and the cheerful comings and goings of people enjoying the place. The rubble tip has also been covered over with earth to become a small hill that gently separates the Fontajau neighbourhood and the park. At one point, the green emptiness of the field gives way to the typical riverbank woods, the dense vegetation of which conceals enthralled waters.

The other visible intervention of the architects is the small bridge connecting the two banks of the park, enabling pedestrians to walk from Fontajau to the centre of Girona. With the latter purpose in mind, it is set diagonally, marking out the most direct route into the heart of the city. It is a high bridge (with possible floods in mind), made with humble, not very decorative materials but its compositional aspect has been delicately approached. The curious passer-by admires this composition with a smile, impressed by the discrete intelligence of these very reserved architects.

This reach of the River Ter is now part of the contemporary city and preserves the spirit of the minor gods of the industrial revolution but, more than anything else, this is a bucolic place, as bucolic as a piece of Renaissance decoration. Today's shepherds

As it runs through the city of Girona, the River Ter has traditionally been of marginal significance. In recent decades, however, urban growth to the north of the river has given it a more central position, a fact that led to the drawing up of a Special Protection Plan that aimed to bring the continuity of this natural corridor into compatible relationship with the new function of a metropolitan park.

The Central Ter Park spreads along the northern bank in front of the Devesa forest. The project has left the wooded area practically intact while intervening in the surrounds of the pavilion where a dumping ground for rubble and a clay pit left a desolate space. In order to avoid the impact that would have been entailed by the construction of a retaining wall in order to channel the watercourse, a gently sloping grassy embankment conceals the quay and pumps that define the riverbed and protect the park's terraces and sports pavilion from flooding. A footbridge improves lateral accessibility, joining Fontajau with the Plaça de les Botxes, which opens into the Rosaleda and the city centre. A weir has been constructed under the bridge, thereby guaranteeing the damming of the water and slightly

Francesc Hereu, watercolour

raising the water table in the Devesa forest and thus improving irrigation of the plane trees. Running next to the water, a fisherman's wharf goes as far as a birdwatching hide in the form of a slightly tilted cube. Scattered over the fields and woods of the park are a number of small constructions used as service buildings or lookouts, by means of which the aim has been to recall, in contemporary language and with materials like wood and concrete, a flavour of ruins and abandoned civil works re-colonised by nature, which is the atmosphere hovering over the Ter, giving it its identity and its beauty. To offer an extreme formulation, one might say that the Central Ter Park is both a hydraulic project and one of atmosphere. The river has ceased to be the city's backyard.

PROJECT **Central Ter Park, Girona, Spain**
DATE **1999**
AUTHORS **Francesc Hereu & Joaquim Español Arquitectes**
PARTICIPANTS **I. Gilabert, Ibering E. P. Ingenieros, D. Arqué, M. Figueres**
DEVELOPER **Girona City Council**
SURFACE **145,000 m²**
COST **2,805,720 €**

and nymphs are the young people stretched out on the grass, the families basking in the sun, the old people going for a stroll, the footballers and runners and the birdwatchers. In the last century dozens of artists and theoreticians repeated thousands of times Michelangelo's maxim: «taking away; this is the sculptor's job». Gottfried Benn was even more radical: «the essence of art is infinite reserve». This is what the architects Hereu and Español think too. The artist has to disappear almost completely, if one wants to hear the inaudible.

Antoni Puigverd, Girona-based writer.

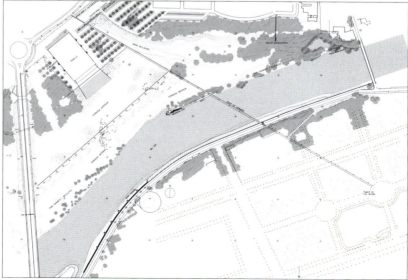

General plan

ACKNOWLEDGEMENTS:

The CCCB wishes to express its appreciation for the contribution of all those people who work, and have worked over the years as members of the European Prize for Urban Public Space team: Magda Anglès, Sònia Aran, avanti-avanti, David Bravo, Cristina Brossa, Judit Carrera, dbloop, Maribel Elizalde, Albert Garcia Espuche, Eva Gimeno, Cristina Hernández, Anna Ibáñez, Anna Llopis, Ciro Llueca, David Lorente, Cristina Mañas, Teresa Navas, Dragan Nikodijevic, Mònica Oliveres, Marina Palà, Judit Prat, Ferran Porta, Rosa Puig, Núria Salinas, Teresa Sieiro, José Antonio Soria, Victòria Torrente and Masha Zrncic.

We are grateful, too, for the permanent support of Viorica Buica, Zaklina Gligorijevic, Hans Ibelings, Maria Llopis, Olivier Mongin, Francesc Muñoz, Carme Ribas, Bashkin Shehu, Elías Torres, Martien de Vletter, Ursula Wahl and Julie Wark, and everyone else who has contributed towards the project and its successful development.

Special thanks are due to the presidents, secretaries and all the members of the juries:

2010
President
Rafael Moneo

Members
Dietmar Steiner
Ole Bouman
Sarah Mineko Ichioka
Francis Rambert
Severi Blomsted
Peter Cachola Schmal

Secretary
David Bravo

2008
President
Manuel de Solà-Morales

Members
Dietmar Steiner
Ole Bouman
Rowan Moore
Francis Rambert
Severi Blomsted

Secretary
Carles Crosas

2006
President
Elías Torres

Members
Dietmar Steiner
Aaron Betsky
Francis Rambert
Severi Blomsted

Secretary
Carme Ribas

2004
President
Oriol Bohigas

Members
Dietmar Steiner
Aaron Betsky
Rowan Moore

Secretary
Elena Cànovas

2002
President
Josep Lluís Mateo

Members
Aaron Betsky
Lucy Musgrave
Dietmar Steiner

Secretary
Joaquim Español

2000
President
Oriol Bohigas

Members
Manuel de Solà-Morales
Philippe Paneral
Michel Bensa
Pierre Pinon
Jan Gehl

Secretary
Albert Garcia Espuche

PHOTOGRAPHIC CREDITS

Front cover: Jiri Havran
Back cover: Anja Schlamann

pp. 50-51: Elías Torres
pp. 54-59: Anja Schlamann
p. 60: Roland Halbe
p. 63 above: Birdseyepix
p. 63 below: Giovanni Torretta
p. 64: Erik Berg
pp. 66-71: Alejo Bagué
pp. 72-77: Manuel González Vicente
pp. 78-81: Ulrich Schwarz
pp. 82-85: Atelier d'Architecture Autogerée
p. 88: muf architecture/art
p. 91: muf architecture/art
p. 91 above, left: David Williams
p. 92: Jason Lowe
p. 93: muf architecture/art
pp. 94-97: Lukas Schaller
pp. 98-101: Vicente del Amo, Jesús Granada, Michele Panella, Jesús Torres García
p. 102-105: Strange Cargo Arts
p. 108: Mladen Radolovic Mrlja
pp. 110-113: Stipe Surac
pp. 114-119: Luuk Kramer
pp. 120-123: Franco Tagliabue
pp. 124-127: Pawel Kubisztal
pp. 128-131: David Baltzer
p. 132: Klaus Overmeyer
pp. 136-139: Eva Serrats
p. 141: Jordi Surroca
p. 141 below: Eva Serrats
pp. 142-147: Hisao Suzuki
p. 148: Julien De Smedt
p. 151 above: Julien De Smedt
p. 151 middle: Hanne Fuglbjerg
p. 151 below: BIG+JDS
p. 152: Jens Schulz
p. 155 above: Aeliane van den Ende
p. 155 below: DS Lansdschapsearchitecten
pp. 156-157: Hélène Binet
p. 160: Joaquín Ponce de León
p. 163 left: Joaquín Ponce de León
p. 163 right: Urbano Yanes
p. 164: Juan Antonio González Pérez
p. 165 above: Juan Antonio González Pérez
p. 165 below: José Ramón Oller
pp. 168-173: Jordi Bernadó
pp. 174-177: Hanns Joosten
p. 178: dS+V Gemente Rotterdam
p. 180: Studio 75B
p. 181: dS+V Gemente Rotterdam
p. 182-185: Carlos A. Sárria
p. 186: David Lorente
pp. 188-189: Barcelona Regional
pp. 192-195: Joan Argelés Cugat, Lluís Casals
p. 198: Dublin City Council
p. 201: McGarry Ní Éanaigh Architects
p. 203-205: Francesc Hereu

www.publicspace.org